P9-DND-387

楽しく
働く。

Joy at Work

Also by Marie Kondo

The Life-Changing Magic of Tidying Up:
The Japanese Art of Decluttering and Organizing

The Life-Changing Manga of Tidying Up:
A Magical Story

Life-Changing Magic: A Journal

Spark Joy: An Illustrated Master Class on the
Art of Organizing and Tidying Up

Kiki & Jax: The Life-Changing Magic of
Friendship

Also by Scott Sonenshein

Stretch: Unlock the Power of Less — and
Achieve More Than You Ever Imagined

Joy at Work

ORGANIZING YOUR PROFESSIONAL LIFE

Marie Kondo

AND

Scott Sonenshein

Little, Brown Spark
New York Boston London

Copyright © 2020 by KonMari Media Inc. and Scott Sonenshein
English translation for Marie Kondo's chapters by Cathy Hirano

Hachette Book Group supports the right to free expression and the
value of copyright. The purpose of copyright is to encourage writers
and artists to produce the creative works that enrich our culture.

The scanning, uploading, and distribution of this book without
permission is a theft of the author's intellectual property. If you would
like permission to use material from the book (other than for review
purposes), please contact permissions@hbgusa.com.
Thank you for your support of the author's rights.

Little, Brown Spark
Hachette Book Group
1290 Avenue of the Americas, New York, NY 10104
littlebrownspark.com

First Edition: April 2020

Little, Brown Spark is an imprint of Little, Brown and Company, a
division of Hachette Book Group, Inc. The Little, Brown Spark
name and logo are trademarks of Hachette Book Group, Inc.

The publisher is not responsible for websites (or their content)
that are not owned by the publisher.

The Hachette Speakers Bureau provides a wide range of authors for
speaking events. To find out more, go to hachettespeakersbureau.com
or call (866) 376-6591.

The KonMari Method™ is a registered trademark
owned by KonMari Media, Inc.

ISBN: 978-0-316-42332-8 (hc) / 978-0-316-49795-4 (large print) /
978-0-316-42973-3 (signed edition) / 978-0-316-42971-9 (B&N signed
edition)

LCCN 2019954682

10 9 8 7 6 5 4 3 2 1

LSC-H

Printed in the United States of America

To my family, my home, and all the things that support me and spark joy in my life — with gratitude.

—M. K.

To my mom and dad:
I finally learned to clean up!

—S. S.

Contents

CONTENTS

CONTENTS

CONTENTS

Notes to the Reader

Although we collaborated on the entire contents of this book, each of us took primary responsibility for half of the writing. Marie's voice is in the introduction and chapters 1, 2, 3, and 11; her name is at the top of those pages. Scott's voice is in chapters 4, 5, 6, 7, 8, 9, and 10, and his name is at the top of those pages. You will also find boxes within each chapter containing the voice of the person not primarily writing that chapter.

The stories and examples from this book are from real people. Sometimes the names have been altered for readability and to protect their identities.

Joy at Work

Introduction

Is your desk always buried under piles of documents? *Yikes! Where's the report I have to submit tomorrow?*

Do you have a never-ending backlog of emails no matter how often you check them? "About the email I sent you yesterday..." *What email?*

Is your schedule packed with appointments with people you don't even want to see?

Are you carrying on like this every day because you've forgotten what you really wanted to do?

Do you find it hard to make decisions?

Are you asking yourself, *Is this all life's about? Just checking things off a to-do list? Isn't there some way to restore order to my job, my career, my life?*

If any of these apply to you, there's one solution: tidy up.

This book is not just about how to tidy up your workspace. It's about how to put in order both the physical and nonphysical aspects of your job, including your digital data, time, decision-making, and networks, and how to spark joy in your career.

Many people feel defeated at the mere suggestion of tidying up. "I can't possibly make time for that! I'm far too busy already," they protest. "There are too many decisions I need to make to even think of tidying," some say, while others claim, "I've already tried it. I sorted all my documents, and now they're just a mess again."

Quite a few people don't believe they *can* find joy in their job. "I'm stuck in useless meetings all day long. Tidying's never going to change that," they insist. "Besides, too many things are out of my hands. There's no way work can be joyful." In fact, however, it's tidying up properly that makes it possible to spark joy at work.

Since the age of five, I've been fascinated by tidying. I pursued this subject right through my school years and went on to take my first steps as a tidying consultant at the age of nineteen while still at university. The KonMari Method arose from my experiences of teaching people how to tidy up.

My approach has two distinct features: it's simple but effective, ensuring you'll never revert to clutter, and it uses a unique selection criterion—choosing what sparks joy. When we ask ourselves, *Does this spark joy?* we reconnect with our inner self and discover what's really important to us. The result is a lasting change in behavior that sets life on a positive track.

I introduced this method in *The Life-Changing Magic of Tidying Up*. Translated into forty languages, it has sold a combined total of more than twelve million copies. For the past few years I've been busy sharing my method worldwide. During this process, one question has come up repeatedly: How can we tidy up the workspace and spark joy at work?

Most people see me as a specialist in tidying homes, not as someone with expertise in tidying workspaces, let alone in career development. While working for a Japanese company, however, I spent most of my spare time teaching company executives how to tidy their offices. Even people at the firm where I worked began asking me for advice. It was because I became so busy with these lessons that I finally decided to quit my job and launch my career as an independent consultant.

My trained consultants continue to offer lessons and lectures on tidying the workplace using the KonMari Method. They share with each other the knowledge and experience they gain and fine-tune the content accordingly. Through this process, it has become clear how much tidying the workplace improves performance and enhances the joy we get from our work.

For example, clients have told us that it has boosted their sales performance by as much as 20 percent, increased efficiency to the point where they were able to leave work two hours earlier, and helped them to reassess the meaning of their job, rekindling their passion for it. We've seen countless examples of how tidying up can improve one's work life, both materially and psychologically. Just as tidying the home sparks joy in our lives, tidying the workplace sparks joy in our work, helping us to become more organized and achieve better results. This book introduces the secrets of that process.

Of course, not everything at work can be evaluated on the basis of whether it sparks joy. There are company rules to follow, superiors who make decisions that affect our work, and coworkers with whom we collaborate. Nor is tidying our physical workspace enough to make our jobs go smoothly. We can truly spark joy in our work life only when we have put every aspect of it in order, including emails, digital data, work-related tasks, and meetings.

That's where my coauthor Scott comes in. As an organizational psychologist and a chaired business-school professor at Rice University, Scott has been at the forefront of research to create more rewarding and joyful careers. His work covers a broad range of subjects, including how to achieve a more positive and meaningful work life, become more effective and productive at work, and problem-solve in business. Based on the results of this research, his bestselling book *Stretch* shows how we can find success and satisfaction at work by making better use of what we already have, whether skills, knowledge, or items. All this makes him a leading expert on how to spark joy at work. Throughout this book, Scott provides cutting-edge scientific research and data on tidying and provides practical lessons on tidying up the nonphysical aspects of work.

In chapter 1, we share data related to tidying that we're sure will get you motivated. Chapters 2 and 3 cover how to tidy your workspace. Chapters 4 through 9 look at tidying digital data, time, decisions, networks, meetings, and teams. Chapter 10 covers how to multiply the impact of tidying at your company. The final chapter transcends the framework of tidying, suggesting actions you can take to spark even more joy in your daily work and the type of mindset and approach that lead to a joyful career. This chapter includes stories from my own experience that are intended to get you thinking about how you can spark joy in your work life.

We hope you'll use this book as the master key to a joyful career.

CHAPTER 1

Why Tidy?

What's the first thing that greets you when you get to the office on Monday morning?

For many, it's a desk covered in things, things, and more things! Piles of documents, random paper clips, unopened letters delivered who-knows-when, unread books, and a laptop plastered with sticky-note reminders. And beneath their desk are often bags of promotional giveaways from customers. I'm sure most people heave a deep sigh at the sight and wonder how they'll ever get anything done when their desk is such a mess.

Aki, an office worker at a real-estate agency, was one of those who suffered from a messy desk. Even though it wasn't that big (the top was only about as wide as her arm span, and it had only three drawers), she could never find anything in it.

Before a meeting, she was always frantically searching for her glasses, her pen, or a folder, and she often had to reprint her documents and materials when she failed to unearth them. Many times she became fed up and resolved to organize her desk, but come evening she would be too tired and put it off until "tomorrow," piling all the documents she had used that day on one side before heading home. Of course, the next day she would end up searching through that pile for the materials she needed before she could even begin tackling her work. By the time she finally got started, she was exhausted. "Sitting at that messy desk was totally depressing," she told me. Unfortunately, she had good reason to feel this way.

Various studies show that messy conditions cost us far more than we could ever imagine, and in multiple ways. In a survey of one thousand working American adults, 90 percent felt that clutter had a negative impact on their lives. The top reasons they gave were lowered productivity, a negative mindset, reduced motivation, and diminished happiness.

Clutter also adversely affects health. According to a study by scientists at UCLA, being surrounded by too many things increases cortisol levels, a primary stress hormone. Chronically high levels of cortisol can make us more susceptible to depression, insomnia, and other mental disorders, as well as such stress-related physical disorders as heart disease, hypertension, and diabetes.

In addition, recent psychology research shows that a messy

environment taxes the brain. When surrounded by clutter, our brains are so busy registering all the things around us that we can't focus on what we should be doing in the moment, such as tackling the work on our desk or communicating with others. We feel distracted, stressed, and anxious, and our decision-making ability is impaired. Clutter, it seems, is a magnet for misery. In fact, the data show that people like me, who get excited by the sight of a messy room and can't wait to tidy up, are the exception.

But it's not just individuals who are affected. Clutter is bad for business, too. Have you ever spent hours looking for something at the office? Or even lost it completely? Almost half of office workers report mislaying one important work-related item a year. It might be a file folder, a calculator, a memory drive, a briefcase, a laptop, or a cell phone. Not only does replacing lost items cost money, but losing them in the first place causes emotional stress and creates unnecessary waste that damages the environment. But the greatest loss is the time spent looking for them. Data show that the search for lost things adds up to an average of one workweek per year per employee. In a span of four years, that comes to a whole month. In the United States alone, this loss in productivity when converted to cash amounts to an estimated US$89 billion annually. This is more than double the combined profit of the world's five largest corporations.

These figures are staggering, but this is the reality. The

effects of clutter can be devastating. Still, there's no need to worry. All these problems can be solved by tidying up.

How Tidying My Workspace Changed My Life

After graduating from university, I got a job at a staffing agency in the corporate sales department. My euphoria at joining the workforce, however, was short-lived. Although it's only natural for new hires to experience difficulties when they first start, my sales performance never seemed to improve. Of the fifteen people newly employed that year, I was always in the bottom three.

I arrived at the office early, spent hours on the phone trying to make appointments with prospective clients, kept those appointments I did manage to make, and made lists of more potential customers in between. In the evening I grabbed a quick bowl of noodles at a shop in our building, then returned to my desk to prepare materials. I seemed to be working all the time, yet I never got results.

One day, after another discouraging round of sales calls, I put down the receiver with a deep sigh and bowed my head. Staring dejectedly at the top of my desk, I realized with a start that it was a complete mess. Scattered around my keyboard were a pile of outdated sales lists, a half-written contract, a paper cup with some tea I hadn't finished, a shriveled-up tea bag, a week-old bottle of water, scraps of paper on which I had scrawled random sales tips from my coworkers, an unread business book someone had recommended, a pen missing its cap, a stapler with which I planned to staple together some papers but had forgotten . . .

I could not believe my eyes. How could this have happened? I had been working as a tidying consultant since I was in university, yet despite my confidence in my tidying skills, I had been so swamped with my new job that I no longer had time to do any consulting and had even become lax in my tidying habits at home. Somehow I had lost touch with my inner tidying geek. No wonder I wasn't having any success at work.

Shocked, I came into the office at seven the next morning to tidy my desk. Marshaling all the knowledge and skills I had honed over the years, I finished within an hour. Soon my workspace was clean and clutter-free. All that was left on my desk was the phone and my computer.

Although I'd like to say that my sales performance shot up immediately, things didn't change quite that fast. I did, however, feel a lot happier being at my desk. I could find the documents I needed right away. There was no mad search for things just before I dashed off to a meeting, and when I came back, I could launch right into the next task. Gradually, I began to experience more joy in my work.

Tidying had been my passion for years, and I already had a strong hunch that tidying up one's home could change one's life. But now it hit me that tidying the workplace was important, too. As I sat at my desk, which felt brand-new, I sensed that keeping it tidy would make my job more fun and help me love my work.

Why Tidying Up Improves Work Performance

"My desk is such a mess, I'm embarrassed," my colleague Lisa confided one day. She worked on the same floor as I did. When she saw me putting my desk back in order, she became intrigued and began asking my advice. She had never been good at tidying even as a child, and her parents' home was full of things. Her apartment, she told me, was a shambles, too. "Not only have I never tidied in my life, it never even occurred to me that I should," she said. But working at an office had made her aware that her desk was far messier than anyone else's.

Her story is not so unusual. A major difference between a home and a workspace is that at work, people can see us. At home, almost no one sees our clothes or books, even if they are strewn all over the floor. But an office is a shared space, which makes the difference between a tidy desk and a messy one obvious to all. Surprisingly, this fact has a much greater impact on our working life than most people realize.

Several studies on employee evaluations in the workplace have shown that the tidier a person's space, the more likely others are to see them as ambitious, intelligent, warm, and calm, while yet another study showed that such people are seen as confident, friendly, industrious, and kind. The list of adjectives makes these people sound like real winners. Moreover, studies show that tidy people tend to gain others' trust more easily and are more likely to be promoted. Beyond the importance of a good reputation for career advancement, research repeatedly finds that we work to the level of expectations that others set for us. Higher expectations boost our confidence and usually result in better performance. This theory, known as the Pygmalion effect, is based on studies showing that students' grades improve when they sense that their teachers expect them to excel. The Pygmalion effect has also been shown to be important in work settings, where employees' performance rises or declines to the level of expectations set for them.

The findings of these studies can be summarized in three simple points. A tidy desk results in a higher evaluation of our character and capacity. This raises our self-esteem and increases our motivation. As a result, we work harder and our performance improves. Looked at in this way, tidying up sounds like a pretty good deal, doesn't it?

After she applied my lessons to her workspace, Lisa's sales performance improved, her boss praised her highly, and her confidence in her job steadily increased. As for me, let's just say that I got high marks within the company for my ability to tidy up, and that made me happy.

Are Messy People Really More Creative?

A bare, tidy desk is sterile and boring. "If a cluttered desk is the sign of a cluttered mind, of what, then, is an empty desk a sign?" These words have been attributed to the creative genius and physicist Albert Einstein. Regardless of whether he actually said them or not, his desk appears to have been buried under piles of books and papers. Similarly, Pablo Picasso painted while surrounded by a jumble of paintings, and Steve Jobs, the founder of Apple, reportedly kept his office cluttered on purpose. Legends of geniuses with messy offices are too numerous to mention. As if to corroborate these, a recent study conducted by researchers at the University of Minnesota concluded that a messy job setting is more likely to generate creative ideas.

Perhaps because such stories abound, people frequently ask me for confirmation. "But a cluttered desk is good, isn't it?" they'll say. "It stimulates creativity, right?" If you're wondering if your cluttered desk might make you more productive, too, and whether it's worth reading the rest of this book, here's a little exercise for you to try. Start by mentally picturing your desk at the office, your studio, or your workplace. Or, if you are sitting there at this very moment, just take a good look around you. Next, answer these questions.

Are you honestly feeling positive about working here right now?

Does working at this desk every day really spark joy for you?

Are you sure that you're giving full scope to your creativity?

Do you really want to come back to this tomorrow?

These questions aren't intended to make you feel bad. They're meant to help you get in touch with how you feel about your work environment. If you answered yes without hesitation to all of them, your joy level at work is impressively high. But if your response was ambivalent, if you felt your heart sink, even a little, then tidying up is definitely worth a try.

To be honest, it doesn't really matter which is better—a clutter-free desk or one that is total chaos. The most important thing is that you yourself are aware of the kind of environment that brings you joy at work; that you know your own joy criteria. And tidying up is one of the best ways to find out. Many clients who have used this method to tidy up their homes end up with a bare and simple interior when they're done, only to realize a little later that they want more decoration. That's when they begin adding accents they love. Often, it is only after tidying up that people realize what kind of environment sparks joy for them.

Are you the type who can tap into your creativity more easily once you've tidied up, or the type who is more creative in the midst of clutter? No matter which you are, the tidying process will help you discover the kind of joyful workspace that makes your creativity bloom.

The Vicious Cycle of Accumulating Clutter

Research shows that clutter decreases the joy we feel at work for two main reasons. First, it overwhelms the brain. The more stuff we have around us, the more overloaded the brain becomes. This makes it harder for us to recognize, experience, and savor those things that are most important to us—the things that bring us joy.

Second, when we are inundated with things, information, and tasks, we lose our sense of control and the ability to choose. No longer capable of taking the initiative or choosing our actions, we forget that work is a means for realizing our dreams and aspirations and lose our love for our job. To make matters worse, when people feel they are no longer in control, they begin to accumulate more unwanted stuff while also struggling with a sense of guilt and pressure to do something about it. The result? They put off dealing with their stuff indefinitely, generating a vicious cycle of ever-increasing clutter.   **S.S.**

The High Cost of Nonphysical Clutter

It is not just our desks that need tidying. We're overloaded with nonphysical clutter, too. In particular, modern technology has generated digital clutter in the form of excess emails, files, and online accounts. Add to this the many meetings and other tasks we need to deal with, and it seems impossible to get things under control. To achieve a work style that truly sparks joy, we need to tidy up every aspect of our work, not just our physical space.

According to one study, a typical office worker spends about half his or her day dealing with emails and averages 199 unopened emails in the inbox on any given day. The Center for Creative Leadership reported that 96 percent of employees feel they're wasting time dealing with unnecessary emails. In addition, almost one-third of programs installed on most computers are never used. It's clear from these examples alone that we're inundated with digital clutter while on the job.

And what about the information we need to use various online service accounts? An average internet user has 130 online accounts per email address. Even considering that some can be combined and managed under one account, such as Google or Facebook, the number of user IDs and passwords needed is still impressive. And just think about what happens when you forget your password. You type in a combination of possible IDs and passwords without success, eventually giving up and changing it.

Unfortunately, statistics show that we're very likely to repeat this experience. According to a survey of workers in America and the UK, the loss in productivity from forgetting or mislaying passwords comes to at least US$420 per employee annually. In a company that employs about twenty-five people, that amounts to more than US$10,000 a year. Perhaps we should set up a "lost password fund" that automatically transfers a donation whenever someone forgets their password and use the proceeds to benefit society.

Meetings also take up a large percentage of our working time. The average office worker wastes two hours and thirty-nine minutes a week in ineffective meetings. In a survey of senior managers conducted by researchers, the majority of respondents expressed dissatisfaction with company meetings, claiming that they were unproductive, inefficient, interfered with more important things, and failed to bring the team closer together. Meetings are held for the benefit of the company, yet ironically senior managers, the very people responsible for organizing them, see them as detrimental. The cost of unproductive meetings comes to more than US$399 billion annually. When I think about this, along with the losses incurred by forgotten passwords and the US$8.9 billion wasted in time spent searching for mislaid items, I can't help wondering how much revenue the government could generate by taxing for this kind of clutter. Crazy, I know, but still...

Scott will share with you the details of how to tidy nonphysical clutter from chapter 4 on. For now, just note that there will be a few hurdles you'll need to tackle to make your work spark joy. That means you've got great potential for improvement. Imagine having organized not only your desk but also all your emails, files, and other digital data, and always being on top of your schedule for meetings and various tasks. Think how much joy this could bring to your work.

Tidying Up Helps You Find a Sense of Purpose

When I was working for a company, one of my colleagues who had started working there two years before I did asked for advice in decluttering her workspace. During our tidying sessions, she told me, "I'm here to work and make a living, not to enjoy myself. Life is more fun if you finish your work quickly and concentrate on enjoying your free time."

Everyone has their own working style and their own way of thinking. I know that some people approach their work in the same way as my coworker, but let me be very blunt. That's a terrible waste. Of course, because we are paid for the work we do, all jobs come with responsibilities. If we work for an organization, there are also many things over which we have no control. As long as we're members of society, it's unrealistic to expect that our personal happiness should always be given top priority. Unlike tidying the private space within our home, tidying up at work doesn't guarantee that everything at our office or in our job will always spark joy.

Still, it seems such a shame to give up and work only out of obligation, making no effort to spark joy in our environment. Next to the home, work is where we spend most of our time, and at some points in our lives, we may even spend more time on the job than at home. Work is a precious part of life. While making good use of our skills, wouldn't it make sense to enjoy our time at work even a little? And if we're going to enjoy it, why not also work in a way that makes others around us happy?

Some of you may be thinking, *That's all very well for you to say, but I hate my job. I can't imagine it ever sparking joy.* Even so, I still recommend that you try tidying up. Tidying can help you get in touch with what you really want, show you what you need to change, and help you find more joy in your environment. That may sound too good to be true, but it's not.

I have witnessed how tidying can transform many aspects of my clients' work life. One client, for example, remembered her childhood dream while tidying up her books and quit her job to start her own company. While tidying documents, a business owner identified a problem in her business and made a bold shift. And another client, upon completing the tidying process, recognized the kind of lifestyle she wanted and switched jobs so that she worked half as many hours. These changes didn't occur because these people were unusual in some way. They were simply the cumulative result of examining each thing in front of them and choosing whether to keep it in their life or to let it go.

"This was supposed to be my dream job, but now I'm scrambling just to keep up with a flood of tasks. I'm always longing to go home early."

"I can't figure out what I want to do. I've tried a lot of different things, but I just don't know what I really want."

"I poured everything into my work to get this far, but now I'm wondering if this is really the right career for me."

If you are having doubts like this about your job or career, now is the perfect time to start tidying up. Tidying is much more than sorting things and putting them away. It's a major project that will change your life forever. The goal of the method shared in this book is not just to have a nice neat desk but to begin a dialogue with yourself through tidying—to discover what you value by exploring why you are working in the first place and what kind of working style you want. This process will help you see how each task you do is linked to a joyful future. In the end, the real goal is to discover what brings you joy in your work so that you can give it your best. We invite you to experience for yourself how tidying up can spark joy in your career.

CHAPTER 2

If You Keep Falling Back to Clutter

S ir, you should really tidy up your desk!"

That's what I once blurted out to a prospective client. It was the summer of my second year with the staffing agency, and my job was to promote our recruitment services. That meant finding out what kind of staff each company needed and introducing the right person for the job. I was in charge of small- and medium-sized businesses. Companies with only ten employees or fewer rarely have their own personnel department, and often the company president is responsible for everything, including hiring. In this case, the person I was addressing was the president. Looking worn and tired, he had just said to me, "I'm so busy, I wish I had a secretary."

Conscious of my role as a human resources recruiter, I asked, "If you hired one, what tasks would you want a secretary to do?"

"Hmm. Let me see," he said uncertainly. "Well, one thing for sure, I'd like someone who could organize my documents and writing tools. You know, someone who would just hand me the right pen when I asked for it. And it would be great if they could tidy up my desk, too."

That's when I started putting my foot in my mouth. "But you can do that yourself!" I exclaimed, realizing my impertinence only once the words were out, not to mention the fact that I'd basically just told him he didn't need a secretary. Another sales opportunity lost!

But he kept right on talking as if he hadn't noticed. The more he said, the clearer it became that organizing was not one of his strengths. He was raised in a family where clutter was the norm, and he was always losing things. On his first job, his boss had told him he was a dead loss at keeping things tidy, a fact about which he still had a complex.

When he finished talking, I asked if he would mind showing me his desk. It was right on the other side of the partition behind which we were meeting. A single glance told me everything. It was just a plain gray desk, but the computer in the center was hemmed in by what looked like futuristic skyscrapers formed by precarious Jenga-like stacks of documents, books, and mail. By this time I was already working weekends as a tidying consultant, and I just couldn't help telling him that he should really tidy up his desk.

That was the start of our tidying lessons. Of course, these

had to take place outside of business hours, so we met early in the morning or after work. By the end of several sessions, his office was neat and tidy. As an added bonus, he was so pleased with the effects of tidying that he introduced me to many other business owners, which meant my sales performance shot up. Thereafter, whenever I visited a new client, I would take a quick look at the boss's desk. Opportunities to slip some tidying advice into the conversations increased and, before I knew it, the number of clients for my consulting business had multiplied.

To be honest, however, among my tidying clients were some who suffered rebound. Not all of them were able to keep their offices tidy after they completed my course. What was the difference between those who succeeded and those who didn't? Their mindset when they started.

The information we work with is frequently updated as we receive new materials and as the content of various projects evolves. Documents and papers quickly pile up. Even if we tidy our desk once, to keep it that way we need to stay on top of it, and that requires a mindset that keeps us motivated, an under-standing of *why* we want to tidy up.

Most people I know who have succeeded in tidying up once and for all have done so on their own initiative. They also start off with a clear idea of who they want to be and what kind of lifestyle they want. By contrast, people who launch into tidying without a clear idea of why they are doing it or, worse, with the hope that they can get someone else to do it for them often revert to clutter even if they succeed in tidying up the first time.

So let me ask you now: Why do *you* want to tidy up?

If you answered that you want to improve your work performance or eliminate stress, that's fine, but to keep yourself motivated, you'll need to be more precise and identify in clear, concrete terms your ideal approach to work and the effects you hope tidying will have on your life. So before you start, visualize your ideal work life.

Visualizing Your Ideal Work Life

Imagining your day at work in concrete detail while asking yourself what kind of work life sparks joy for you and what values are important in your work is the first step to tidying, and it's crucial to success.

Whenever I think about this topic, I'm always reminded of an email I received from Michiko, a client who had finished tidying up. She worked for a medical supplies manufacturer, and before she started the tidying process, her desk was always piled with papers layered like a millefeuille pastry. The subject line of her email was: Ideal Work Life Achieved! In it she wrote:

> By the time I reach the office in the morning, I'm already excited. There is nothing but the phone and a potted plant on my desk. I take my laptop

and cord from their designated spot on the shelf and set them up. Placing the coffee I bought on the way to work on a favorite coaster, I freshen the air with a spritz of mint aroma mist, take a deep breath, and get to work. Everything is in its place, so I waste no time searching, and it only takes a second to put each thing back where it belongs when I'm done. Two months have passed already, and even I can hardly believe I still feel this happy every morning.

Michiko's email, which exudes happiness, reads like a textbook case of a joyful work life. I'm sharing it here because it contains all the keys you need to visualize your own ideal. The trick is to imagine in vivid, motion-picture detail what your whole day will look like after you finish tidying up. That image should include three elements: the physical environment, your behavior, and your feelings. Visualize what your workspace looks like, such as your neat and tidy desk and where everything is stored; what you do there, including such things as enjoying a cup of coffee or refreshing aromas; and what you feel when you do that: for example, excited, fulfilled, or content.

To paint a realistic picture of your ideal work life, these three elements should be treated as one set. The most important, however, is imagining what you feel when you're in your ideal workspace. Try closing your eyes and seeing yourself as you arrive first thing in the morning. If nothing pops into your mind, imagine the scene that Michiko described when she reached her desk and then observe what you're feeling. Did your heart leap? Did you feel a warm rush of pleasure spread through your chest?

When we imagine each detail, right down to the physical response our emotions generate, instead of just thinking about them intellectually, our ideal becomes almost tangible. This naturally reinforces our desire to attain that state, helping us to stay motivated.

There's one other important aspect to consider when visualizing your ideal work life—the time frame. Think of the flow of your day: getting to work in the morning, taking time for a break, finishing work, leaving for home. Imagine what your workspace looks like at different points during the day. When we examine our ideal from different angles like this, we begin to see the concrete steps we want to take next, from adding more color to making our filing space more accessible, and that boosts our motivation even further.

Picturing your ideal work life is essential for tidying nonphysical clutter, too. When decluttering your email, for example, visualize how you would like to handle incoming mail and then consider how much mail in your inbox would work best for you. When tidying time, visualize the amount of time you require for each type of job and how you will feel when doing it. Reexamine these ideals from different perspectives, such as productivity, efficiency, and your relationships with the members of your team. Only when you have set tidying goals based on a clear picture of your ideal work style can you approach tidying with the right kind of mindset.

An Exercise to Identify What Sparks Joy at Work for You

Do you find it hard to visualize your ideal work life? If so, here's a quick exercise to help you identify your own personal joy criteria. Read each of the twelve statements and then, using a scale from 1 to 5, rate your level of agreement or disagreement with each one. There's no right or wrong answer. Just listen to your heart and respond honestly. (1=strongly disagree, 2=disagree, 3=neither, 4=agree, 5=strongly agree)

_____ I get a lot of pleasure from learning new things.

_____ I seek out challenges at work.

_____ I benefit by working with others who have more skills or expertise than me.

_____ TOTAL

_____ I would like a flexible work schedule.

_____ I like to feel safe speaking my mind at work.

____ I want freedom to do my work as I best see fit, without too much supervision.

____ TOTAL

____ I want to maximize the amount of money I make.

____ I would like to master my job.

____ I value earning praise from people I work with, such as colleagues, customers, or supervisors.

____ TOTAL

____ I prioritize forming genuine friendships at work.

____ I enjoy helping others at work.

____ I prefer to have colleagues working closely with me, versus working independently.

____ TOTAL

Add up your answers for every three questions. This means you will have a total score for questions 1, 2 and 3, and 4, 5, and 6, and so on. The first three questions focus on learning, the next three on work freedom, the following three on achieving, and the last three on connecting with others. Your scores show how much you value each of these areas. Areas with a score of 12 or higher are ones you value particularly highly.

> So what aspects are most important for you? Once you've identified them, you can use them to help you visualize your ideal work life.   **S.S.**

Tidy Up All in One Go and You'll Never Rebound

"I've tidied my desk a million times, but before I know it, it's a mess again."

Rebound is one of the most common problems people consult me about. Anyone who has tidied has likely experienced it at least once. Take, for example, my coworker Jun. "I reorganize my desk quite often, you know," she said as she showed it to me. "It may not seem like it, but I actually don't mind tidying."

When I see a desk that appears neat and tidy, I give the top a cursory glance and then check those places that are out of sight. I start with the drawers. Pulling them open, I'm often greeted by an array of unused pens, old business cards, a jumble of paper clips and erasers, ancient lip balm, a package of stale gum, supplements, plastic cutlery, paper napkins, and single-use packets of ketchup and soy sauce that probably came with a takeout lunch.

Next I roll back the chair, crouch down, and peer under the desk. Reaching in, I haul out the cardboard boxes and paper bags that are shoved underneath. They're usually stuffed with books and documents, as well as clothes, shoes, and snacks. My actions are met with looks of surprise. "You mean I should tidy underneath my desk, too?" people ask. But organizing just the top of your desk is not enough.

If you want to tidy up so completely that you never revert to clutter again, aim for one simple goal: knowing where everything in your workspace belongs. What kinds of things do you have and how many? Where do you keep them? What types of items tend to increase due to the nature of your work, and when that happens, where will you put them? Only once you have a solid grasp of all these things can you say you've tidied up.

How can you achieve that? Tidy your entire workspace by category, all in one go. If you tidy the top of your desk today, the first drawer tomorrow, and another the next day, throwing out things little by little when you have time, you'll never put your space in order. The first step is to set aside a block of time for tidying. Then, gather all the items you have by category and decide which you should keep and which you should discard. Once you've done that, decide where to store the things you are keeping. To tidy up properly, follow these steps in that order.

Scott and I explain how to tidy physical and nonphysical aspects by category in detail from chapter 3 on. For now, just keep in mind that the key to success is this: Tidy by category, quickly and completely, all in one go. Whether tidying your workspace or tidying your home, this is the essence of the Kon-Mari Method.

It may sound hard, but don't worry. Tidying the physical workspace is much simpler than tidying a home. For one thing, workspaces are far smaller with fewer categories, making it easier to decide what items to keep and where to keep them. And it takes much less time. To tidy a home using the KonMari Method takes a minimum of three days for a person living alone without too much stuff, and anywhere from a week to several months for a family, depending on how much they own. Tidying up just a desk, on the other hand, takes an average of five hours and, depending on the type of work, can take as little as three. Even for someone who has more space, such as their own cubicle or room, it usually takes only up to ten hours. So if you can set aside two days, you should be able to finish tidying the physical aspects of your workspace.

If it's a real challenge to make time for tidying—if you can't set aside a block of five hours straight—try splitting the process into several sessions. The most common pattern among my clients is to come to the office two hours before work starts and complete tidying in three two-hour sessions. One thing I've noticed is that those clients who schedule their tidying sessions close together develop a rhythm that helps them finish quickly. So if you don't have much time to spare, I recommend keeping your tidying sessions close together so that you can maintain intensity. To drag out the process to the point where you have to keep starting is a complete waste of time, making this the most inefficient approach to tidying up.

When I say tidy up "quickly and completely, all in one go," I mean within about a month. Although some people are surprised that it's okay to take this long, a month is not long compared to the number of years most of them have put up with a cluttered desk. Although it would be great to finish within one or two days, if it takes longer, that's not a problem. The important thing is to give yourself a deadline. You can decide, for example, that you'll aim to finish by the end of the month and then schedule specific time slots for tidying. If you just tell yourself you'll tidy when you have time, you'll never finish.

Tidy up properly, all in one go, then designate a place for every single item. Once you know where everything in your workspace is stored, you can keep track of your things even when they start to multiply. That's what makes it possible to keep your space tidy. By learning the proper way to tidy up, anyone can achieve a joyful workspace and never rebound.

Choosing What to Keep

Does this spark joy?

This question is the key to the KonMari Method. It serves as a simple but very effective tool for tidying the home—a personal, private space. We take each item in our hands and choose only those that spark joy, letting go of the rest.

But what about for a workspace? Jobs require things like contracts, outlines of upcoming meetings, and company IDs, which don't particularly spark joy yet can't be discarded, as well as utilitarian items like tape, staplers, and paper shredders, all of which you use but have no authority to discard if you don't happen to like them. When you take a good look around, you're likely to find that your desk is ugly, your chair is boring, and even the cover of the tissue box in the office's shared space doesn't inspire you. The more you look, the more obvious it becomes that you can't choose what to keep at work based solely on what sparks joy for you. But before that thought throws a bucket of cold water on your passion for tidying, let's go back to basics.

Why do you want to tidy up?

No matter what your ideal work life is, the final goal is the same: to be able to work with joy. So when tidying up, what matters most is to choose things that contribute to your happiness and appreciate what you keep.

There are three types of things that you should keep. The first are things that spark joy for you personally, such as a favorite pen, a memo pad with a design you like, or a photo of your loved ones. The second type are things that are functional and aid your work, things you use frequently like staples or heavy-duty packaging tape. They don't particularly spark joy, but they make your daily work easier. Just having them lets you relax and focus on your job.

The third type are things that will lead to future joy. Receipts, for example, don't inspire much of a thrill, but they have the obvious merit of allowing you to be reimbursed when you use them to claim expenses. Papers related to a project about which you feel little enthusiasm will, if you complete that work conscientiously, be a plus for your career. And if being valued for your reliability is part of the dream you want to realize, this will also bring you future joy.

So remember these three categories: things that directly spark joy, those that provide functional joy, and those that lead to future joy. These are your criteria for choosing what to keep in your workspace.

If the words *spark joy* just don't seem to click in your work setting, feel free to substitute something else that does. To give just a few examples, I know a CEO who used, *Will this help my company prosper?*, a bank teller who used, *Do I feel a buzz of anticipation?*, and a department manager and baseball fan who used, *Does this belong on the first team, the farm team, or out of the team's plan?*

What matters is whether the item you have taken in your hands will play a positive role in your work. Always keep in mind that the reason you are tidying is not to throw things away and declutter your desk but to realize your ideal work life, the one that sparks joy for you.

Choosing What to Discard Is Very Different from Choosing What Sparks Joy

If you're thinking that choosing what sparks joy is the same as choosing what to discard, think again! Although deciding what to keep and deciding what to discard may sound like different sides of the same coin, from the perspective of psychology they are worlds apart. To choose what sparks joy is to focus on the positive aspects of the things we own, while to choose what to discard is to focus on the negative.

Data show that negative emotions have a more powerful impact on our thoughts than positive emotions. A study examining 558 words for different emotions in English concluded that 62 percent of them were negative, compared to only 38 percent positive. In another study, participants from seven countries (Belgium, Canada, England, France, Italy, the Netherlands, and Switzerland) wrote down as many emotions as they could think of in five minutes. People from all seven countries recalled more negative words than positive ones. In addition, among the most used words, only four were shared by all seven countries, and of these three were negative: *sadness*, *anger*, and *fear*. The only word expressing positive emotion shared by all seven was *joy*.

As this example illustrates, the human brain gives greater weight to negative than to positive experiences. If we focus on the negative when we discard, the best we can hope for is to eliminate what we don't like. Not being sick isn't the same as being healthy, not being poor isn't the same as being rich, and not being sad isn't the same as being happy. Likewise, getting rid of things we don't like isn't the same as choosing things that spark joy.

So when tidying, focus on the positive—on the things you love. If you do, you'll likely find that you actually enjoy tidying. **S.S.**

Create an Environment Where You Can Focus

The only sounds in the hushed office are the tapping of fingers on keyboards and the murmur of me and my client in the middle of a tidying lesson.

"Does this spark joy?"

"Yes."

"Is this important?"

"No, I don't need that anymore."

"What about this document?"

My client's voice drops to a whisper. "Ah, that's about someone who quit the office last year. There was a bit of trouble, you see."

"Oh, sorry."

I learned an important lesson during this session with my client when I first began teaching business executives how to tidy. In a quiet office, a tidying lesson can seem quite loud, and it's hard to talk without disturbing others. My poor client must have felt a bit uncomfortable.

When tidying up your workspace, it's important to create an environment that helps you focus. If you tend to worry about what others might think, timing will be an important concern. If you can access your workspace on holidays or have your own cubicle or room, you'll have more options about when to tidy. But if you work in an open office and need to tidy during the week, you will probably have to do it before or after work if you don't want to bother others. As for me, I made it my routine to conduct lessons from 7:00 to 9:00 in the morning before my clients began their working day.

Tidying first thing in the morning has many benefits. When you know you'll be starting work at 9:00, you will tackle tidying with concentrated efficiency, and because you're still fresh, you'll feel more positive about what you're doing and enjoy the process. In this condition, deciding what to keep and what to discard goes smoothly. That's why for many years I advised my clients that early in the morning was the best time to tidy their workspace. Recently, however, my view has begun to change, thanks to the experience I've gained through sharing my method in other countries.

In Japan, it's quite common for people to stay late at the office, which makes it hard to focus on tidying up after hours. But at many of the companies I've seen in America, there's almost no one left in the office after six at night. And on Fridays, the number of people starts dwindling gradually from about three in the afternoon. In such cases, it's quite possible to focus on tidying up even after work.

I noticed another difference, too. Most Americans I spoke with told me that it wouldn't bother them at all if someone tidied up their space during the working day, regardless of the noise that person made. To make sure they understood what I meant, I asked, "Even if it was a totally exposed, open office that was really, really quiet?" I still got the same answer. Clearly, in America, how to tidy up one's office discreetly, a problem I had been studying for years, was less relevant.

In Japan, it's considered polite to care about what others think and to be careful not to bother them. I'm sure that's true in America and most other places, too. Through this experience, however, I learned that what bothers people is not the same everywhere. When we tidy, the important thing is to create an environment in which we feel comfortable so that we can focus on tidying. That might mean picking a time when fewer people are at the office or just letting our coworkers know that we'll be tidying up. Or we could even invite our coworkers to join us. In fact, I recommend wherever possible that the whole company tidy up at the same time.

A Japanese publisher I know set aside one day at the end of the year for each employee to tidy their desk area. Apparently this cleared the air and improved the atmosphere in the company so much that it went on to produce multiple bestsellers. Tidying improves the work efficiency of every individual involved and fosters a positive attitude, so it makes sense that it would have great results. Even if it's not possible to involve the whole company, wouldn't it be wonderful if an entire department or members of the same working group decided to tidy up together?

Let Your Tidying Festival Begin!

Once I began offering tidying lessons to business executives, my life became much busier. On weekdays I provided tidying lessons from seven to nine in the morning, then worked hard at my sales job from nine thirty until quite late in the evening. On weekends I offered home-tidying lessons. In conversations with my coworkers, I would mention that I had helped a client finish tidying her kitchen over the weekend, or that a business executive had gotten rid of four garbage bags full of papers that morning. It wasn't long before everyone in the company knew that I was involved in the tidying business, and requests for tidying lessons from my coworkers and superiors increased.

My days were full and satisfying, but I never dreamed that tidying would become my profession. My colleagues thanked me by taking me out for a meal, and even though I accepted payment from clients outside the company, I saw these tidying lessons as a side business, not a regular job.

One day, however, a client who had completed my lessons turned to me as I stood with him admiring his perfectly tidy desk and said, "You should really be spreading this tidying method to everyone. You're the only one who can do that, you know." These words made me realize that many people long to tidy up and, most importantly, that I love helping them to do that. That got me thinking about going independent, and in the end I quit the company to focus on my work as a tidying consultant.

I have since gained a great deal of experience in consulting. During that process, I've noticed several rampant misconceptions about tidying. For example, most people believe that tidying is an arduous chore that must be done daily for the rest of their lives. Perhaps some of you think so, too, but there are in fact two types of tidying: daily tidying and festival tidying. The first involves putting things you have used during the day back in their place and identifying where anything new you have acquired belongs in your storage scheme. A tidying festival, on the other hand, means reassessing everything you own, asking yourself whether each item is truly important in your life now, and organizing your own storage system. I call this process a "tidying festival" because it is tackled intensively and completely over a relatively short space of time.

In the workspace, a tidying festival means reexamining not only every physical thing in that space but also all the nonphysical aspects as well. For example, tidying your email involves examining the kinds of mail you keep in your inbox, while tidying time involves identifying how much time you spend on each activity. Doing this gives you a complete picture of what you have and how much, and, as you look at the items in each category one by one, you can identify which ones you should keep and where they belong or which should be given priority.

Both kinds of tidying are important, but without a doubt, a tidying festival has the biggest impact on our lives. That's why I recommend finishing your tidying festival first before thinking about how to keep your space tidy on a daily basis. If you tidy up properly all in one go and experience a neat and orderly workspace, your body's cells will remember just how pleasurable such an environment is. This feeling will naturally inspire you to keep your workspace that way. Of course, this approach applies to tidying not only the physical but also the nonphysical aspects of your work, such as digital data and networks discussed from chapter 4 on. First, assess your current situation, then choose what you really want to keep, and experience the joy of working in a tidy space.

So let's get started. Begin by asking yourself what kind of

work life sparks joy for you and picturing it vividly in your mind. Then let us help you launch your own tidying festival, which will make that ideal a reality. With the right mindset and the right approach, you can achieve the working life you have always dreamed of.

CHAPTER 3

Tidying Your Workspace

First, let's look at the concrete steps for tidying up your physical workspace. Tidying the nonphysical aspects will be addressed in subsequent chapters.

Whether you work at a desk or have your own cubicle or room, the basic steps of the KonMari Method for tidying the physical workspace are the same.

To begin with, tidy only those spaces for which you have sole responsibility. This is a cardinal rule of tidying, and it basically means starting with your own desk. If there are any communal spaces, for example a storage area for supplies, a break room, or a meeting room, just ignore them for now, even if they aren't as tidy as you'd like them.

If you work at home, deal with work-related items separately from personal items. For example, if some of your books and documents are work-related while others are not, identify only the work-related items for now and focus on tidying them, leaving personal items for a later date when you are ready to tidy your home.

If you have your own studio or workshop, the principles are the same, but depending on how much stuff you have, tidying may take longer. For example, if your workspace is the size of a large garage, if your cupboards and shelves are full of tools and parts, or if you have a large volume of products or artworks on hand, give yourself longer, perhaps even two months, to complete the tidying process.

The order in which you tidy is important in the KonMari Method. In the home, I generally recommend starting with clothes and progressing through the more advanced categories in the order of books, papers, *komono* (miscellaneous items), and sentimental items. I recommend this order because starting with the easiest and working up to the hardest category helps us develop our capacity to choose what to keep or let go and decide where to store everything. For tidying the workspace, just drop the clothes category and proceed through books, papers, *komono,* and sentimental items.

The rules for tidying these categories are also the same. Work on one category at a time. Begin by taking out every item in each category or subcategory and piling them in one spot. For example, if you are working on the *komono* subcategory of pens, take all your pens from the drawers and penholders and place them on top of your desk. Then choose which ones you want to keep. This process gives you a clear picture of exactly how much you own in each category, making it easier to compare and decide which ones to keep or discard. It also makes the next step of storing by category easier.

Points to keep in mind for storage are outlined on pages 56–58. You can wait until you've finished choosing what to keep from every category before you start storing, or you can start as soon as you finish choosing what sparks joy from one category and continue doing the same thing for each category as you go along.

Once you've grasped these basics, it's time to tidy your desk by category.

Books: Discover Your Values Through Tidying

A bestseller that you hoped to read someday, a how-to book about accounting you bought to improve your skills, a book received from a client, a business journal distributed by the company . . . What kinds of books do you have in your workspace?

Books are filled with valuable knowledge that can help us do our jobs. When kept at our desk or on our bookshelves, they can give us inspiration or a sense of security. Reading them during lunch or coffee breaks can boost our motivation, and just displaying them can add a personal touch to our workspace. In reality, however, we often keep books at work for the wrong reasons.

One of my clients had a bookcase in her office filled with

unread books. When we counted them, there were over fifty, and more than half had been sitting on the shelf for two years or more.

"I'll read as many as I can during my next vacation," she declared. When we met again, however, I wasn't surprised to hear that she had given up partway through. Most of the books that she had managed to read were her most recent purchases. "To leave them unread seemed such a waste that I decided to speed-read to get through them," she said. "But I began to feel like I was just doing it out of a sense of duty. It wasn't bringing me any joy. This seemed even more of a waste, so I decided to let a lot of them go."

In the end, she decided to keep only a carefully selected fifteen in her office. Just like us, books have a peak period in their lives. That's when they should be read, but it's quite common for people to miss that timing. How about you? Do you have any books at work that are past their prime?

When tidying up your books, begin by gathering them all in one spot. Perhaps you're thinking it would be better to just choose them by looking at the titles while they're still in your bookcase, but please don't skip this step. Books that have stayed too long on the shelf have become part of the scenery. Your mind doesn't register them, even when they are directly in your line of sight, and that makes it hard to decide which ones spark joy. Only by taking each one in your hands can you actually see them as separate entities.

If you find it hard to judge whether or not a particular book sparks joy, try asking yourself certain questions. For example, when did you buy it? How many times have you read it? Do you want to read it again? If it's a book you haven't read yet, visualize yourself when you first purchased it. That memory can help you decide if you still need it. If it's one that you planned to read "sometime," I recommend setting a date by which you will do so. Without conscious effort, "sometime" never comes.

Another question to ask yourself is what role that book plays in your life. Books that spark joy are those that motivate and energize you when you read and reread them, those that make you happy just to know they're there, those that bring you up-to-date on the latest information, and those that help you perform your work better, such as manuals. In contrast, books that you bought on impulse or because you wanted to impress people, as well as those that were gifts but that you doubt you'll ever read, fulfilled their purpose the moment you bought or received them. It's time to let them go with gratitude for the joy they gave you in the past.

One last question to ask is whether you would still buy that book now if you saw it in a bookstore, or if it has passed its prime in terms of your interest in it. Just because you paid for it doesn't mean that you must finish reading every book you own. Many books fulfill their purpose before they're ever read, particularly those on the same topic bought at the same time. These are the ones you should thank for the joy they sparked when you bought them and then bid them farewell.

The purpose of asking such questions isn't to force yourself to mindlessly purge your books. Rather, it's to help you explore your relationship with each one you possess. The awareness you gain will help you decide whether or not a book will bring you joy if you keep it.

Sometimes people ask me how many books they should keep, but there's no fixed number. For books, and for other categories, too, the amount that feels right will differ for each individual. The real benefit of tidying up is that it helps you identify your own personal standard. If books spark joy for you, then the correct choice is to keep as many as you want with confidence.

Storage space at work, however, is often limited. If at any time you feel yourself veering away from your ideal work life because you have too many books, stop and adjust the number in whatever way is least stressful for you. You could place them on a shelf designated by the company for used books, take them home, sell them to a used-book store, or donate them to schools, libraries, hospitals, and so on.

Tidying books is a powerful means of self-discovery. The ones you choose to keep because they spark joy reveal your personal values. One of my clients, Ken, was an engineer. His goal at the start of the tidying process was an orderly space where he could work more efficiently. When I asked him to describe his ideal work life, he wasn't sure, although he thought it might be nice to go home earlier.

As he went through his books, however, he found that he had many on self-development and particularly on how to lead a more fulfilling life and find more passion in one's work. This showed him that he longed to enjoy his job more and achieve self-fulfillment through doing his best. Such insights helped him to regain his love and passion for his work. So you see, tidying up is really an epic voyage of self-discovery.

Papers: The Basic Rule Is Discard Everything

After books, the next category is papers. Dealing with papers is usually the most time-consuming part of tidying a workspace. Even today, when smartphones and tablets have become ubiquitous and the number of paper materials has significantly decreased, people still tend to have a lot of paper.

The rule of thumb for papers is to discard everything. My clients always look dumbfounded when I say this. Of course, I don't mean that we should eliminate papers entirely. I'm just trying to get across how much resolve we need in order to choose only those that are absolutely necessary and to discard the rest. There is nothing more bothersome in our workspace than papers, which seem to accumulate before we realize it. Sheets of paper seem so slim, we often hang on to them without really thinking. Yet when we need to sort them, that process becomes time-consuming because we have to make sure we know the content. Worse, the more papers we accumulate, the more time it takes to find particular documents or reports, and the harder they are to put in order. For this reason, I recommend setting aside a block of time on your calendar just for tidying papers.

As with the other categories, start by gathering all your papers together in one spot and looking at each one. Papers are the only category that can't be selected by asking yourself if they spark joy. Instead, you must check the content. Even papers that are in envelopes should be taken out and checked page by page in case advertising leaflets or other unwanted material are mixed in with them.

It can be helpful to sort papers into categories while you are skimming through the content. This makes filing them when you're done quicker and easier. Papers can be broadly divided into three categories: pending, save because you have to, and save because you want to.

The pending category includes papers that need some kind of action, such as outstanding bills and project proposals that must be reviewed. I recommend storing all of them in one upright filing box until you've dealt with them. That way they won't become jumbled up with papers in other categories.

Next, let's look at papers we're required to save. Compliance laws dictate that we must keep certain types of reports, statements, contracts, and other documents for a specific period of time, regardless of whether or not they spark joy. Sort them by category and file them in a filing cabinet or in file folders on a shelf. If you don't need to keep the originals, you can also scan them and store them electronically (see chapter 4). In this case, rather than scanning them as you sort, it's more efficient to put them in a "to-be-scanned-later" pile and do the scanning all in one go. There are pitfalls to scanning, however, which I discuss on pages 58–59.

The last category is papers you want to save for other reasons. These might include documents you want to keep as a reference or ones that actually spark joy for you. Whether or not you keep these is entirely up to your discretion. But because rebound is a common problem when people hang on to things "just because," keep in mind that the basic rule for papers is to discard them all.

In my tidying lessons, when a client has trouble deciding which papers to keep and which to discard, I fire off questions about each one—things like "When do you need this?," "How long have you had it?," "How often do you go back and look at it?," "Can you find the same content on the internet?," "Have you already saved it onto your computer?," "How much of a problem would it be if you didn't have this?," and "Does it really spark joy?"

If you find yourself struggling over whether or not to keep a particular document, don't let yourself off lightly. Don't waste this precious opportunity. Ask yourself tough questions and commit yourself to tackling your papers so thoroughly and completely that you'll never have to tidy on such a massive scale again. If you balk at the premise that you should discard them all, try imagining that I have just walked into your office and announced that I'm going to shred all your papers. What would you do? Which ones would you scramble to save from the shredder?

Depending on the type of job, you may find that you can discard almost all your papers. A high-school teacher told me that she digitized any that were essential, completely emptying two filing cabinets and increasing her efficiency, too.

One business manager I knew made it a habit to decide whether he needed a document as soon as he got it. He shredded it on the spot if he didn't and never again had a problem with papers piling up. But we do need to be cautious when using a shredder. That same manager became so quick to use it that he shredded a resignation letter from one of his employees, envelope and all. (He was actually my former boss and the letter he inadvertently shredded was mine.)

How to Store Papers So You Never Rebound

Some who have read this far may now be feeling anxious. Even if you tidy up, papers are bound to pile up again quickly, making rebound inevitable. But there's no need to worry. As long as you follow the three rules of storage I introduce below, you'll never return to paper clutter.

Rule 1: Categorize every paper down to the last sheet.

Start by sorting your papers into clear categories, such as presentations, project proposals, reports, and invoices. Or you could sort them by dates, projects, or the names of individual clients, patients, or students. One of my clients, for example, designated files for Design Ideas, Management Ideas, English

Study, and Documents to Keep and Remember. Use whatever system works best for you.

The most important point is never to store even a single sheet of paper "just because." Now is the time to categorize your papers in a way that makes your work easier. Make sure every paper is sorted into a category.

Rule 2: Store your papers upright.

Do you know people who are always asking, "Where did that file go?" Often it's because they are piling their files in stacks on their desk. There are two disadvantages to stacking documents. First, it's difficult to determine how much you have, so you don't notice how much you are accumulating over time and end up with a messy desk. Second, you forget about the files at the bottom of the pile and waste time looking for them.

For optimal efficiency, it's crucial to store your papers in a hanging-file system. Put each category of papers in a separate folder and store them in a filing cabinet or upright in a filing box placed on a shelf. Storing them this way makes it easy for you to see how many papers you have. It also looks neat and tidy.

Rule 3: Make a pending box.

Make a pending box, in which to keep only those papers that you need to deal with on that day. Again, I recommend using an upright filing box so that you can clearly see how many papers need processing. If you prefer, you can use a tray-type filing box and store them flat, but be sure not to forget the existence of the papers on the bottom. When you've processed pending papers, discard those that don't need to be kept.

Just as for tidying anything else, tidying up your papers makes them incredibly easy to manage because you know exactly how many of each type you have and where they are. Once you have sorted your papers and decided where each category belongs, look at your workspace and determine the maximum amount of space you have available for storing them. When you exceed this storage capacity, papers will begin to overflow. That's a signal that you need to reexamine what's there. Check for papers that no longer need to be saved, and let them go. By checking regularly like this, you can keep your papers tidy at all times.

Beware the Scan Trap

Scanning is so convenient. There's nothing easier than scanning a document you have decided to discard and saving it as data. But this very convenience can sometimes be your downfall.

One of my clients told me he wanted to scan important pages of his books before discarding them, but it took him much longer than he expected. During that time, he realized that scanning them didn't spark joy, so he decided to take photos with his smartphone instead. But this also took more time than he expected, and in the end, he decided to discard his books without saving anything. As for the scanned and photographed pages that he had taken such pains to record, he didn't look at them once.

To give another example, the owner of a dentistry clinic kept setting aside papers to be scanned before discarding them during our tidying lessons. He barely made a dent in the overall number of papers, while the number to be scanned kept increasing. Shoved into paper bags in the corner of his office, they remained there for a month, then two, then three. There was no way he could tidy up at that rate. A year later, I visited his office and was quite shocked to find that the pile of bagged papers he had set aside for scanning was still sitting there, untouched. Realizing that he had not used any of the papers in those bags for a whole year, he began going through them, taking out only those that were absolutely necessary and discarding the rest.

Of course, some important papers need to be scanned, but before you start, ask yourself whether you really need to keep a record of all the papers you've set aside for scanning. It's important to keep in mind not just how much time it takes to scan these materials but also how much time you'll need to sort and store the scanned data. If you have an assistant to do that kind of work for you, that's one thing, but if you'll be doing it all on your own, it could consume an enormous amount of time. If you still want to save things by scanning, then make sure to allocate specific blocks of time for it in your tidying schedule. If you just tell yourself you'll scan those materials when you get a chance, it will never get done.

Tidy Your Business Cards and Review Your Relationships

Do you ever look at a business card and wonder who on earth it belongs to, unable to even conjure up a face? This happens surprisingly often when tidying. I always encourage my clients to take this opportunity to discard, but many people feel guilty throwing business cards away. In Japan, some of my clients hesitate because they believe such cards carry a piece of a person's soul. But if they're that precious, rather than shoving them into a drawer and neglecting them forever, it would make more sense to treat them with respect, thanking them for the work they've done, and sending them off in a way that protects the personal information they contain.

When sorting business cards, gather them all together and look at them one by one. One business owner I advised had four thousand business cards. Soon after we started our lessons, he discovered that he didn't need any of them because he was connected with almost everyone on social media. He also had the email addresses of anyone with whom he had communicated by email. He discarded almost all of his cards, scanning a few that he needed to keep, then chose about ten that sparked joy just because they belonged to people he admired.

You can also say goodbye to the business cards of people you've already been in touch with through email or social media. If you don't have time to input the info into your contacts folder right away, record their email addresses in your computer or phone by scanning or taking a photo. It's worth taking advantage of new technology for storing, too, such as apps that use your phone's camera as a scanner to record business-card data in your contacts list.

As for me, when I recently tidied my business cards, I was left with just one—my father's. I kept it because he has worked at the same company for more than thirty years. Every time I look at it, I'm vividly reminded of how he has provided for our family all these years through his work. I couldn't part with it, so instead, I gave it a place in my desk.

If just having some cards inspires or energizes you, keep them with confidence.

Divide *Komono* into Subcategories

"There's no end in sight! I feel like giving up!"

"I'm so confused."

"I'm going crazy!"

When clients start sending me desperate emails like these, they are almost always in the middle of tidying *komono*. This is, after all, the category with the largest number of subcategories. Stationery supplies, hobby *komono,* household supplies, kitchen *komono,* foodstuffs, bathroom supplies . . . Just listing them is enough to make your head swim. But don't worry. The number of *komono* subcategories in an office is far fewer than the number in a home, and if you have already succeeded in tidying up your documents and papers, you can and will conquer *komono,* too.

If you approach *komono* calmly at your own pace, you'll quickly get an overall picture of what types you have. Common subcategories found in a typical workspace include the following:

Office supplies (pens, scissors, staples, tape, etc.)

Electrical (digital devices, gadgets, cords, etc.)

Job-specific *komono* (product samples, art materials, supplies, parts, etc.)

Personal-care items (cosmetics, medicine, supplements, etc.)

Food (tea, snacks, etc.)

Begin by gathering all items in the same subcategory in one place and pick them up one by one. If your drawers are so jammed with stuff that it's hard to see what's there, pull them out and dump the contents on your desk or the floor. In this case, you can pick out those things you wish to keep as you are sorting them into subcategories.

Office Supplies

Office supplies can be divided into two types: desk supplies and consumables. When tidying this subcategory, tidy each type separately.

1. Desk supplies: These include things like scissors and staplers, of which you generally need only one. People who don't know what or how much they have usually have more than they need. One of my clients, for example, had accumulated three pencil sharpeners, four identical rulers, eight staplers, and twelve pairs of scissors. When I asked him why he had so many of each, he responded vaguely that he had lost the first one so bought another, didn't realize he already had so many, or thought it would be handy to have one close at hand. With desk supplies, you need only one of each item for your workspace, so select one and say goodbye to the rest. If your company has a supplies-storage area or communal workspace, you could put them there.

2. Consumables: These include things that you keep on hand and use up, like sticky notes, paper clips, notebooks, stationery, and cards. Although we may need to keep a few extra in stock, is it really efficient to have a mountain of sticky notes overflowing your drawers or a cache of ten red pens? Think about how many of each you actually need at your desk—for example, five packs of sticky notes or thirty paper clips—then set aside the number you decided was adequate and return the rest to wherever your company keeps office supplies.

Electrical

When tidying up electrical *komono,* it's quite common to find broken appliances or gadgets that are now obsolete. Is there any point in keeping such things in your desk? Some people's drawers are stuffed with multiple pairs of earphones or charger cords from defunct smartphones. This might make sense if they were planning to open a used-cord store, but do they really need them all? Some cords are so random that even the person who owns them no longer knows what they were for. There's only so much space to store things in your desk. Now is your chance to figure out what those cords are and say goodbye with gratitude.

Job-Specific Komono

We all have things that are unique to our professions. It might be paints and canvases for artists, beads and wire for accessory designers, or cosmetic samples from manufacturers for beauty-column writers. Depending on the profession, the volume may be overwhelming or the content may seem uninspiring. But precisely because these items are directly connected to our work, they have the most potential to spark joy in our lives once we start tidying and to keep us motivated to the finish.

Take, for example, Leanne, an artist who found that oil paints didn't spark joy, despite being precious tools of her trade.

She changed mediums, creating a new style. There was also an illustrator who launched a new career in costume design after discovering her love for textiles, and a pianist who was in a slump but regained her passion for music when she parted with some old music scores. I often hear similar stories. For many people in creative professions, choosing only those things that spark joy seems to fill them with inspiration, fueling their creativity. Physical tidying and making more space for yourself gives you more room in your mind, allowing new ideas and creativity to flow.

Pick up each item in this subcategory and ask yourself if it sparks joy. If you pay attention to your feelings, you should feel a surprisingly clear answer. The cells in your body will either leap with joy or sink like lead.

Personal-Care Items

Personal-care items include hand cream, eye drops, supplements, and other things that help us perform our work with greater ease. Sitting at the office for hours can cause stiff shoulders, a sore back, and eye fatigue. Having care products on hand to ease such physical distress makes us happy.

Kay, a client who worked for an advertising agency, loved relaxation aids. During our tidying sessions, we found lots of these on her desk and in her drawers, including scalp massagers and disposable eye masks. When asked, she explained that she needed them to help her relax because her work was so busy. "This product isn't even sold yet in Japan," she said proudly. "And this facial equipment is going to be a hit, I think." She was clearly obsessed with these things.

Intrigued by the sheer volume, I asked her to tell me how she used them all. Her answer, however, came as a surprise. "I use this aroma oil when I miss the last train and need to calm myself down," she said. "And this herbal eye mask is for when I've been at the computer ten hours straight. This massage ball is great for getting the kinks out. I put it on the floor after everyone has gone home and lie on top of it. It feels fantastic!"

Her explanations were thorough and detailed. The more I listened, the clearer it became that regardless of all these relaxation items, her work situation was shockingly hard. I couldn't keep myself from asking, "But does working like that spark joy?"

In the end, she reduced her overtime and took more than half of these items home. Now she enjoys using them to unwind when she gets back from work. "Thinking about my ideal work life, I realized that I would be happier using them to relax at home, not at the office." There was more color in her cheeks, and she looked much less stressed.

No matter how wonderful the personal-care products you keep at work, if your work life itself doesn't spark joy, you're putting the cart before the horse. Start by imagining your ideal work life, then decide what kinds of personal-care products will help you realize that ideal. And what kind won't.

Snacks and Food-Related Items

One client who worked for a media company had such a huge stash of ketchups and salt packages, napkins, and plastic forks from takeout food that it took up half a drawer. Until she started tidying, however, she was oblivious to how much she actually had. Finding out was a shock.

Are you accumulating things like snacks, candy, and gum at your desk? If so, check the expiration dates and set a limit on the number you will keep on hand from now on. This is your chance to say goodbye to surplus stock and put your desk in order.

Incidentally, while giving tidying lessons in American companies, I discovered something in this category that would never be seen in a Japanese office. Can you guess what it was? Alcoholic beverages. It may not be true for every American company, but at the ones I visited, quite a few employees kept some at their desks. Considering that Japanese workers would never drink at the office, this was quite an eye-opener for me. Learning about different cultural characteristics is what makes tidying up in other countries so fascinating.

Sentimental Items

This last category is the hardest because it consists of things of sentimental value, such as photos and letters. That's why it's left to the end. As you tidy up all the other categories, you learn what you really value and hone your ability to choose what sparks joy.

As with the other categories, start by gathering all the items together in one spot. Take each one in your hands and ask yourself, *Will this spark joy for me if I keep it at my desk now?* If your response is that it once supported you in your work but you no longer need it, thank it for what it gave you, and let it go with gratitude. Taking this opportunity to reflect on how each item has allowed you to do your job effectively makes tidying up all the more meaningful. If you have too many items that spark joy to keep them all at your desk, take some of them home. You can speed up the process if you put such take-home items aside in a bag while you're tidying. Just remember to take the bag home when you're done.

For those who find tidying up sentimental items difficult, try taking a photo before letting them go. When Scott tidied up his office, he found it hard to say goodbye to letters and pictures from his daughters. Taking photos of them helped him to part with them. He now reserves the spot where he kept them for his daughters' latest contributions, making that space more joyful.

Snap a Picture and Then Discard!

Research has shown that taking a photo of sentimental items can be effective in helping people to discard them. In one study, researchers advertised a donation drive using two different posters that were placed in different dorms. One urged students merely to collect and donate their sentimental clutter, while the other urged them to take a photo of it first and then donate it. Over 15 percent more items were donated from students living in dorms where the advertisement instructed them to take a photo first.   **S.S.**

Desk Storage

Once you've chosen only those things that spark joy, it's time to store them. There are three basic rules of storage.

Rule 1: Designate a place to store each item and store by category.

The reason people rebound after they have gone to all the work of tidying up is that they don't decide where each item belongs. Because they don't know where to put things after they've used them, their space gets cluttered again. That is why you will want to decide where to store each item. It's so much easier to keep things tidy if you get into the habit of immediately putting each item back where it belongs.

It's important not to scatter storage for things in the same category. Storing everything in the same category in the same place lets you see at a glance how much you have. This has added benefits. Once you know what you have, you no longer accumulate excess or buy unnecessary items.

In a general office setting, it's common to store business cards and stationery supplies in the top drawer; electrical, personal-care, and food-related items in the second drawer; and documents and papers in the third drawer. This is the basic storage layout for a typical office desk, but it will vary depending on the type of desk you have or the type of tasks your work involves. Make adjustments as needed and create a space in which you feel comfortable working.

Rule 2: Use boxes and store things upright.

The amount of storage space in a desk is very limited, so you'll want to maximize its effectiveness. Boxes are great for this. You can use boxes of various sizes as drawer dividers. Store items in the same category in one that suits their size and shape, such as a small box for items like flash drives and a medium-sized box for personal-care items like supplements. Small things in particular store better when they are arranged upright in a box rather than placed directly in a drawer with no dividers. The box keeps them from disintegrating into an anonymous heap and lets you see at a glance where things are when you open the drawer.

Any type of box that fits in your drawer will do. You can buy boxes specifically for this purpose or use empty ones you have on hand in your home. I often use business-card boxes and smartphone packages. They're just the right dimensions to fit inside a desk drawer, making them very easy to use. The trick is to store everything standing upright as much as possible. This not only looks neater but maximizes the available space. All items that are the right height should be stored upright. I even store erasers and packs of sticky notes in the upright position.

Rule 3: As a rule, don't store anything on top of your desk.
Your desktop is a work surface, not a storage cupboard, so the rule of thumb is to store nothing on it. Pick a spot in your drawers and on your shelves for each item or category. As much as possible, the only things on your desk should be whatever you need right now for the project you are working on. Keep this image of a clear desktop in your mind when you start storing. People who do so usually finish with only a laptop and an ornament or potted plant on their desk.

Designate a storage space even for things you use daily, such as a pen or memo pad. My clients are often surprised to find that it's not inconvenient at all to store these things out of sight when not in use. Once they experience how a neat and tidy desk enables them to focus on their work, they quickly become addicted to that state.

Of course, this doesn't mean that your desk must be completely bare. If you find it easier to work when you have all your writing tools in a pen stand on your desk rather than lined up in a drawer, then that's where you should store them. What matters is the approach. We should assume that we will keep nothing on our desk, and then choose very thoughtfully any items we feel will spark more joy or make our work easier if they are on top.

To sum up, store by category, use boxes, and don't store anything on top of your desk. Keep these three rules in mind as you design your storage. Decide where every item belongs and know exactly what you have, down to the smallest items.

How Tidying Up Can Change Your Life

Above, I have outlined the steps for tidying up your physical workspace for each category. I hope you find these useful. If you're still feeling anxious because there seem to be so many steps, or because you have failed to successfully tidy up despite many attempts, don't worry.

I have helped many people to tidy up their workspace. Even those who boast that they really have nothing to throw away find that they reduce two-thirds of their stuff just through taking everything in the same category out of their desk, holding each item in their hands, and asking themselves if it is really worth keeping. Clearly, there is a huge gap between what we think might be necessary and what we actually feel is worth keeping when we confront each item individually.

Similarly, although many people are convinced that they have so much stuff it will take them at least half a year to tidy their desk, it's quite common for them to finish in less than a week once they get started. As you can see, there is a big difference between imagining what tidying will be like and actually doing it. That's precisely why it would be a waste to read this book and not try it, especially if you feel that something clicks. Only by trying it can you experience the true value of tidying up.

But what is its true value? I think it's far more than feeling fantastic about your nice clean desk or seeing your work efficiency improve. Tidying up allows you to rediscover your own self. When you face each item you possess, one by one, and ask yourself if it sparks joy or if it will contribute to a joyful future, you begin to see quite clearly what you really want and what makes you happy. By the time you have finished tidying, your mindset, your behavior, and the choices you make have changed. As a result, your life undergoes a dramatic transformation. I have seen this happen for countless clients, but here I would like to share the story of Mifuyu and how, through tidying up, she made a major discovery about herself that changed her life completely.

Mifuyu's Life-Changing Experience

Mifuyu was a successful marketing rep for a luxury fashion magazine published by a major Japanese publishing firm. As you would expect of someone in that field, she received a generous salary and wore all the latest fashion brands. Her brilliant career inspired envy in many of her peers. But for some reason, she had a nagging feeling that something wasn't quite right, that she was trying to be someone she wasn't. She decided to take tidying lessons because she wanted to find her true self.

Mifuyu started with her home, choosing what to keep on the basis of what sparked joy. To her surprise, she discovered that she felt no joy at all for the $2,000 jacket or the designer dresses hung carefully in her closet. Nor was she drawn to the stiletto heels that she had barely worn. Instead, she wanted to keep only those clothes in which she felt totally comfortable, such as a plain white T-shirt and jeans and a simple navy shawl, the texture of which she loved. In the end, she kept just one-fourth of all the things she owned.

Impressed by the effect tidying had on her life, Mifuyu decided to try tidying her workplace. The next weekend, she went into the office when no one else was there. As is typical for people who work in publishing companies, there were magazines and manuscripts scattered on top of her desk, and her drawers were stuffed with papers. After four hours of intensive tidying, however, her workspace looked brand-new, as if she had just started working there. All she kept were two clear files of pending material, some stationery supplies, and three books.

On Monday, her colleagues stared at her desk, stunned by its transformation. "Are you planning to quit?" they asked. But the person who was most surprised was Mifuyu herself. And she was particularly amazed by the transformation she experienced in her life. For one thing, she was far more stable emotionally. Not long before, she had been diagnosed with depression due to overwork and had had to take sick leave. Tidying up, however, seemed to have restored her emotional equilibrium, and she was able to work with purposeful composure.

Before, when things went badly at work, she felt as if she were on an emotional roller coaster. She would either blame the situation and other people, telling herself, "It was just bad timing," or "It's because he said that," or put herself down, constantly fretting over and berating herself for past mistakes. After tidying, however, she was able to accept her mistakes constructively, telling herself that next time she would try to do things differently and even feeling grateful for the learning opportunities they gave her.

These may sound unrelated to tidying, but many people who finish tidying up experience such changes. To face the things we own through tidying is to confront our past. There will be times when we regret our purchases or feel embarrassed by our decisions. But to face these feelings honestly and let things go with gratitude for teaching us what we really need is to acknowledge our past choices. By constantly repeating the mental process of identifying what we truly want and deciding what to do on the basis of what brings us joy, we acquire a positive perspective that affirms every choice we make.

"I knew that my actions were my own responsibility," Mifuyu told me. "But before tidying up, it was hard for me to accept that the situation confronting me was the result of my own choices. I was convinced that I was incapable of making the right decision when it really mattered. However, as I faced my possessions one by one, I began to see things differently. I decided not to think so hard, to live more simply, and to make what sparked joy the guideline for all my choices. I realized that being responsible for my actions really meant being true to myself in the way I lived my life. I think that helped me to relax and be more flexible."

Mifuyu's work speed also improved dramatically. Before tidying, she thought deadlines were made to be broken and always finished her work at the last minute. After tidying, however, she was able to complete her work well ahead of the deadline. "I almost never waste time now searching for things. Even if I don't have a document I need, I can either borrow it from a colleague or download it. It's much faster and more efficient to see immediately that you don't have something and take appropriate action than it is to search your desk forever without even being sure that what you're looking for is there." Her life is much less stressful now that she no longer wastes time on such things.

There's another reason her work speed has accelerated. She used the KonMari Method not only to tidy her home and office but also to tidy her data, such as the contacts in her cell phone, her relationships, her work content, and her time, choosing what to keep on the basis of whether or not it sparked joy or was essential for the ideal lifestyle she envisioned. As a result, she dropped jobs she didn't need and established a working style focused solely on what she believed really mattered.

Three years later, Mifuyu had become a TV commentator on the national news and the author of several books. She quit the company to work freelance, realizing her long-cherished dream of becoming independent. In Japan, she is a shining example of a woman who has established her own distinctive working style. She travels the world with just a smartphone and a computer, working only on jobs she really likes with people she really likes. Her lifestyle itself provides content for her writing. By tidying up both her physical and nonphysical workspace and choosing only what sparked joy, she sparked joy at work in the true sense of the word.

From Tidying the Physical Aspects to Tidying the Nonphysical Aspects of Your Workspace

Like Mifuyu, many people who finish tidying up their physical workspace want to reexamine the nonphysical aspects of their work, such as the digital data in their computer and the email in their inbox, as well as their networks and their use of time. When people have tidied up their physical space by choosing what sparks joy and experienced how liberating it is to work in a neat and orderly environment, I think it's a natural response to want to tidy up everything else.

But how can we do that? By applying the principles of the KonMari Method introduced in chapter 2: envision your ideal work style, tidy by category, set a clear deadline, and tidy up quickly and completely, all in one go. When choosing what to keep and what to let go, refer to the criteria introduced on pages 37–38: things that directly spark joy, those that provide functional joy, and those that lead to future joy.

That said, each of the nonphysical categories has certain unique features when it comes to tidying. Scott addresses these in detail in chapters 4 through 10, while I share a few of my own thoughts on tidying digital data, time, networks, and decisions, as well as meetings, teams, and culture, subjects we can't avoid if we are to spark joy at work in our collaboration with others.

If the list of nonphysical categories sounds overwhelming, don't let that stop you. Once you get started, you'll be amazed to find yourself eager to apply your tidying skills to other areas of your life. That's how huge an impact tidying can have. So fix that image of a joyful work life firmly in your mind and forge ahead.

CHAPTER 4

Tidying Digital Work

Tony, a marketing professional at a UK-headquartered energy company, used to waste a lot of time figuring out where to save and find digital documents. Across the network, Microsoft apps, his computer's hard drive, and collaboration programs such as Yammer, his digital documents were a mess. The nonstop flow of emails, texts, and voicemails that consumed so much of his time only made things that much more unbearable.

Tony's technology had taken over his work day (and evenings and weekends!) and he needed to do something. He took the bold step of changing his voicemail message:

Your voicemail will not be heard. Please send an email, and your request will be prioritized and responded to accordingly.

Sure, there were plenty of other ways people could reach him, but he finally felt more in control at work. The change emboldened him to move on to his email. He couldn't unplug from email without getting fired—who can? So he did what he could. He processed every email in his inbox daily to prevent them from piling up. He responded to simple requests the same day and took care of everything else within a week. He's now a lot happier at work—and his colleagues noticed. What at first felt radical became adopted by many of his coworkers.

There's plenty of advice out there about how to manage your email and organize your files and smartphone. There's also a lot of variety on what feels right when it comes to managing our digital lives. Jobs come with different technology requirements. In some companies, a specific type of messaging software is a must. For certain professions, such as medicine and law enforcement, always staying connected is a must. You have to find what works for you so you can stick with it. When you tidy your digital life, your main goal is to find a way to gain more control over technology.

For most people, digital life has three main parts: digital documents, such as reports, presentations, and spreadsheets; emails; and smartphone apps. All three share the same problem: it's easy to save everything, so that's what we do—so much so that we feel like we lose control over the technology that's meant to help us. And unlike physical items, we don't notice digital items piling up until it's too late—we've run out of storage space, can't find something, our device slows to a crawl, or we're bombarded with nonstop notifications. It doesn't need to be this way.

In order to get a handle on your digital life, go category by category, starting with documents, followed by emails, and finally smartphone apps.

You Don't Need a Lot of Folders for Your Digital Documents

Start with the "Documents" area on your hard drive or network drive, and its underlying folders, which will contain most of your digital documents. Afterward, tackle your desktop. For other folders found on most computers, such as ones for pictures or videos, you can use a similar approach described here on these categories, too. Now, within the "Documents" area, including its underlying folders, examine each file and ask yourself:

Do I need this document to get my job done?

Will this document provide me with guidance or inspiration for future work?

Does this document spark joy?

If the answer is no to all these questions, delete the document.

You may remember the contents of the document just from the file name, but you may need to open it. If a subfolder shares files on a topic that you're not keeping, go ahead and delete the entire subfolder.

I don't want to get you in trouble, so be sure to follow any document policy at your organization, or any industry standards around keeping files. If you can't technically delete files, move them to an archive area outside your main documents area. Although they will still take up storage space, the files will be separated from those you actively want to keep. With less visual distraction, it will be easier to find what you need.

Regardless of industry or organization, most people can delete draft versions of documents and completed to-do lists, as well as empty their computer's recycle or trash bin. I clear out mine on the last day of every month.

Show Gratitude for the Items That You Are Letting Go

Let go of your digital data with gratitude, as we do for material possessions. Rather than thanking each and every file, just turn on your "thank-you switch" and maintain that feeling while sorting your digital clutter.

The point is to say goodbye to each piece of data, down to the most insignificant file, with gratitude for the role it played in your life. As long as you can do that, you don't need to worry about doing anything else.   **M.K.**

Search technology has improved so dramatically that it makes organizing your documents much easier. Research shows, however, that people prefer to find their files by navigating through folders rather than searching for them. There's something comforting about knowing exactly where a digital document gets stored. Even if you primarily search for files, it's important to organize your digital material. If you have too many files scattered all over the place, you may get false hits in your searches. You don't want your search for a "deck" recently presented to a client to return hits from your latest home-renovation project! And if you have many similar versions of a document, figuring out the most current one can be a struggle.

Create a handful of main folders to minimize the amount of thought that goes into where to put or find something. Then you can use the search tool within a folder to quickly locate what you need. Everyone's job has different requirements, but the three main folders I use should fit many types of work.

Current projects, with a subfolder for each project. (You should try to keep these to no more than ten. After all, how many of us are simultaneously working on more than ten projects? If you are, you'll learn in the next chapter how to tidy your time.)

Records, which contain policies and procedures you regularly access. Usually, these files are provided by others and you typically don't modify them. Examples include legal contracts and employee files.

Saved work, which consists of documents from past projects that you'll use in the future. Examples include files that can help you with new projects, like a presentation from a previous client that can be a good template for a future one. Other types of saved work can include research you've done that could be helpful later, such as benchmarking of competitors or industry research. You may also want to save some projects to have a portfolio to show to prospective clients or new employees for training purposes.

If you keep personal files in the same space, add a "Personal" folder so you don't intermingle personal and work files.

Keep digital documents organized. Staying organized is much easier once you have a small set of intuitive, primary folders. If you decide to keep a new file, put it in the most appropriate folder. Otherwise, delete it. The usefulness of your folders will improve as you consistently place similar files in the same place and keep only what you need. When projects are done, decide whether they warrant being moved to your "Saved Work" folder or if you can discard them. There's no need to store records such as company policies if they're accessible in other places or won't be needed again.

Use the Desktop to Delight

Your desktop should be a special place, but for many people it's a dumping ground. Desktops are often littered with downloaded files used once, old pictures, or forgotten documents. I used to store so many files on my desktop, I couldn't even read the file names! Every time I logged on I was greeted with a visual mess, and just about everything on the desktop was no longer useful.

Transform your desktop into a place that helps you get your work done and sparks joy.

The desktop can include pending documents you need to process, such as reports to read, presentations to work on today, or unpaid invoices. I also place a "Spark Joy" folder on the desktop. For me, this might include files such as a research publication I'm really proud of, a recent teaching evaluation, or a video clip from a speaking engagement. I refresh these items as I publish new papers, teach new classes, or take on new speaking clients. I also keep a recent family picture. Finally, select an inspiring wallpaper to provide a joyful backdrop.

Marie's Computer Desktop

The only things I keep on my desktop are a folder marked "Storage" and any items, such as photos, that I want to use that day.

I consider my computer desktop to be a workspace, just like my desk, so I display only those things that I intend to use right away. My storage folder is like a filing

---

cabinet. Inside are two folders, one called "Documents" and one called "Photos," as well as a document I need to review soon and photos that I'll be using within the next few days. The "Photos" folder contains photos I would like to use in near-future projects.

The "Documents" folder contains documents, Power-Point presentations, and PDF files. I love to sort and orga-nize, so in my case I have a separate folder for each of these categories, but to be honest, there's no need to go that far. You can easily find any document by searching for keywords.

It's the "Photos" folder for which categories are cru-cial. When downloaded, photos usually have unrecog-nizable names that are hard to search for, but it's unrealistic to change each one. That's why it's best to separate them into folders according to use. In my case, I have folders for photos I want to save for work, such as "Tidying Photos" and "Book Covers," as well as folders labeled "For Instagram" or "For My Blog," in which I temporarily store pending photos that I delete when I'm done.

The joy sparked by a tidy desktop can be quite addic-tive. But I must confess that I only started keeping mine tidy recently. One day a fan came over to talk to me while I was working on my laptop at a café. I was so mortified by how cluttered my display was that I've kept my desktop tidy ever since.

How you categorize your digital folders will depend on what's easiest for you in your line of work. The above ideas are just tips for your reference.   **M.K.**

Don't Let Email Take Over Your Work

We send and receive way too many emails—you know that already. But you might not realize how bad the problem is. The typical office worker spends about half his or her day working through emails, and research finds that more than half of employees believe that email interferes with getting work done. That was certainly the case for Sasha. Like many small-business owners, the branding consultant felt the need to be constantly available to clients. She stressed out about checking email so much, it interfered with her sleep—and her business. "I was spending so much time trying to wade through email and staying organized that it was seriously stalling my growth and productivity," she confided.

Research finds that the more time you spend on email, the lower your productivity and the higher your stress levels. Sasha knew it was true for her, so she started scheduling time on her calendar for when she'd respond to clients' messages—and then avoided email the rest of the day. She let her clients know about her email "office hours." At first, she worried they'd be upset and feel like the service level dropped. In reality, everyone was better off. Sasha got much-needed time to focus on her real work, and her clients got fewer and more focused emails from her.

I know it's tempting to check email all the time. I feel that way, too. I worry I'll miss something important, and there's a part of me that thinks being responsible means always being responsive. But I like to remind myself that I have other obligations, which are usually more important. If you're constantly tempted to read and reply, make your own email office hours and give yourself space to enjoy your job without interruption— even if it's just turning off email for thirty minutes a day.

———

Studies find three main ways people tend to approach email. All three can lead to problems.

Some people constantly clean their inbox. These **frequent filers** are always on alert for inbound emails, and when they receive a message, they jump right into action. They put down what they're doing, read the message, and then file it away immediately. Here's the problem: a single email interruption can require twenty-six minutes to pick up where you left off.

Frequent filers end up doing even more harm if they also

use an elaborate and fragmented folder system. Besides taking up a lot of time to maintain, this system makes it hard to find anything and burdensome to file emails away. Indeed, research shows that having more than twenty folders is too complicated to manage. With too many folders, we spend a lot of time finding the right folder to store messages, and then remembering where we put them.

A second way people handle email is to purge their inboxes every few months. These **spring cleaners** go through cycles of cluttered email where they can't find anything, followed by brief periods of near-empty inboxes after they deleted most messages. It's the worst of both worlds—living in clutter and then losing important messages. I know it sometimes creates a rush when you instantaneously go from a full to an empty inbox. That rush will turn to frustration just as quickly if you mistakenly delete an important message.

A third approach is to just let email accumulate in the inbox. These **no filers** don't know how or don't want to put in the effort to manage their email. They are left relying on their email program's search function. Search technology is pretty good, but it works a lot better, and faster, if it's not sifting through mounds of irrelevant messages.

Managing email doesn't have to be complicated—or time-consuming. Simply keep only what's needed for the future and store email in a logical set of a few folders.

Start with your inbox, which is a temporary space for emails waiting to be processed. It is not for storing emails you want to keep permanently, nor is it for housing every email you receive.

When deciding whether to keep an email, ask yourself:

Do I need to keep this email to get my job done in the future? (Sometimes we need to revisit an email exchange or need documentation of a conversation.)

Will reading this email again provide knowledge, inspiration, or motivation for future work?

Does this email spark joy?

Find an approach that makes sense for you and your job. As with digital documents, aim for a reasonable number of folders—typically ten or fewer, including subfolders. Because you can search emails, if projects are related, you can store them in the same folder. For example, if you have projects such as "Blog," "Instagram," and "Facebook," you can create one folder called "Social Media" to include various social media projects.

Other useful folders might include record-keeping folders, such as policy emails from your manager. I also like to keep a joy folder, in which I store emails that I read when I'm having a bad day—emails from students thanking me for a great class, praise for my research from other scholars, and compliments from clients about my consulting or speaking engagements. If there's an important attachment you want to keep, it's usually better to save the attachment to the appropriate folder with your other digital documents.

After you've cleaned your inbox and filed emails away, turn to any existing folders. Start by identifying folders worth keeping. It will be incredibly time-consuming to examine each email if you've been saving every message. Discard folders that aren't needed anymore—for me, that's classes I've previously taught. Again, make sure you're following any organizational or industry requirements about data retention. Also, leave your "Sent" folder as is. It remains searchable, and it isn't worth the effort to selectively examine each message in it.

Finally, process your emails on a daily basis. When new messages come in, shift from thinking everything gets kept to thinking everything gets discarded, unless there's a good reason to keep it. It's best to schedule email work in a few sittings each day, such as at the beginning and end of the day. You will find that something you thought you needed to respond to in the morning gets resolved by the end of the day. Using blocks of time for email will also minimize distractions and allow you to focus on the work that matters most to you. Let people who depend on you know your system and provide another way for them to contact you for highly urgent items so you aren't forced to check email constantly.

Now, you might think that the method I outlined above will never work for you. You're a no filer and tell yourself, "I have neglected my email for so long, I'm a lost cause." If you're over-whelmed, I've got a simple trick for you. Take all your emails and dump them into an archive folder. The folder will be searchable if you need to retrieve anything, even if it will return false hits. Then make a fresh start to keep only what you want and organize emails going forward using a select group of fold-ers, aiming for no more than ten. Confused that in this digital world, you're getting a pass to move digital clutter from your inbox to a storage place? I'll take giving you a greater sense of control over your digital life than perfectly tidy email, if that's more joyful for you.

———

No matter your email approach, we can all agree that getting fewer emails is a good thing. Don't confuse your email with your work. Email is one of many tools to get your job done, but it is not the work itself.

Start with newsletters and mailing lists. You subscribed to them — maybe to help you become better at your job. It's the moment of truth: Which ones really help you achieve your ideal work life and which are just another distraction? Tidy on the premise that you will unsubscribe from all of them and keep only those that spark joy for you. Do the same for any email newsletter you receive after you tidy.

Next, reduce the number of emails you send others. Just because sending an email is easy doesn't mean you should do it. You'll also set a good example for others by sending only the emails necessary to get work done. And by sending fewer emails, you'll likely get fewer responses.

Send emails to only those responsible for an action or who need to be consulted or informed. Don't go crazy copying everyone on an email. If it's appropriate, talk with colleagues, ask if they want to be included on an email chain, and get to know people's preferences. Pause for a moment before copying someone on a message and be honest with yourself: Are you adding someone to an email because they truly need to be informed or you need a response from them? Those are good reasons. Don't copy someone to shame or accuse them in a group setting or to make yourself seem more important.

Be especially careful with the "Reply All" button. If you have a clarifying question that is applicable only to the sender, then ask the sender only. Don't be the person who accidentally clutters everyone's inbox by RSVPing to the entire group about your evening plans.

Marie's Inbox

When I see a huge backlog of emails, it always makes me think of a mailbox bursting with letters.

The only emails I keep in my inbox are those that are pending, such as emails requiring a reply or some kind of

---

action, or ones that I want to read thoroughly later. To keep the volume manageable, I limit the number of pending emails to fifty, the maximum number that can be displayed without scrolling. If I need to save any of them, I put them in a few simple folders labeled "Work," "Personal," and "Financial." Emails are particularly easy to find with the search function, so there's no need to make a lot of categories.

I delete emails I don't need right away, such as newsletters I've finished reading. "Spam" and "Trash" are deleted automatically after thirty days, but it makes me restless when emails pile up, so sometimes I delete everything from these folders manually. Perhaps I'm a bit extreme in my approach, but even feng shui practitioners say that tidying up your inbox will bring you the information you need when you need it. If you notice that you haven't been getting good information in a timely matter, or you want to increase your luck at work, I really recommend tidying up your inbox. **M.K.**

Fewer Apps on Your Phone Means Fewer Distractions

The average person uses a smartphone eighty-five times a day, adding up to more than five hours. There's a reason for that.

Many apps are specifically built to be addictive and can distract us from getting work done.

Here's the shocking thing. The mere presence of a smartphone can make you perform poorly, even if it's sitting, silenced, on your desk. In one experiment, researchers instructed participants to put their phones in one of three places: on their desk, in their pocket or bag, or in another room. Then they asked all participants to complete the same tasks, which included doing math and a simple memory test. The phones were all silenced for notifications and, when on the desk, turned facedown. This made it impossible for any of the participants to be aware of whether they'd received a message or alert.

When the researchers examined the results, they found something surprising. The more accessible the smartphone was—most accessible meant sitting on a person's desk—the worse they did on the math and memory tests. The presence of a smartphone actually made them perform poorly! The researchers reasoned that simply knowing that the smartphone was nearby was distracting and mentally exhausting, even though the phone was completely silenced and the screen was not visible. Thinking about what you might be missing on your phone or wondering what else you could be doing if you held your phone takes up mental resources. In another study, having a smartphone during an exam lowered students' grades. Yes, smartphones can aid productivity, but when we're too attached to them, they interfere with our work. Silence all but the most essential notifications, and keep your phone out of sight when it's not needed. Turn it off during meals and keep it far away at night. And you don't need to take your phone with you everywhere you go. A recent study found that nearly three-quarters of Americans take their phones with them into the bathroom. Trust me, the email, text, or notification can wait until after you flush!

If you had fewer apps on your phone, you'd have fewer distractions and reasons to keep it nearby. Although it's exciting to download the latest app, for most people the default is to never delete an app, even when it's no longer needed or doesn't spark joy. By cleaning up your apps, you'll save space and preserve battery life for those apps that spark joy.

Now pick up your phone and go through each app. First, ask yourself: *Is this app a requirement?* Some companies require certain apps for all employees or for specific jobs, so you'll need to keep these.

Next, ask yourself: *Does this app help me work better?* Whether it's a productivity app or an expense-management tracker, keep apps that make you better at your job or bring you closer to your ideal work life. Don't make excuses to keep apps, such as *I paid for that app* or *One day it might come in handy.* If it's been sitting on your phone dormant for months, you're not going to wake up one day and finally use it.

Lastly, ask yourself: *Does this app spark joy?* Keep apps that you truly enjoy using.

After thinking through these questions, if you discover an app is not worth keeping, let it go. If for some reason it's needed in the future, it's easy to download again and you typically don't have to repurchase it.

After you've slimmed down your apps, it's time to divide them into different categories and organize your screen. When you divide them into categories, think about what purpose each app serves and how often you use it. One approach is to put the most frequently used apps together, on the home screen. Another is to divide apps among a few folders such as "Productivity," "Company," "Social Media," "Travel," and so on. If you don't have many apps, you can simply divide them into "Work" and "Home." Because we each use our phones differently, there is no single best approach here.

Marie's Apps

The home screen on your smartphone can actually be an important source of joy if it's kept clutter-free. I keep frequently used apps, such as my mail, calendar, and photo apps, on the home screen and put the rest into three folders named "Business," "Life," and "Joy." I have only about ten apps showing, and I make it a point to divide them up among three different screens and line them up at the top. That way I can see what really sparks joy for me every time I look at my phone: photos of my daughters.

It's far more fun to tidy when we focus on how to make our smartphone screen spark joy rather than on what a mess it is. **M.K.**

———

Remember, you're the boss of your technology. Let technology advance your work life and help you see more clearly how your work can be a source of joy. When you tidy your digital documents, emails, and smartphone apps, you'll start to realize that these are just tools to help you work, not a storage depot that archives your entire professional life!

CHAPTER 5

Tidying Time

Christina's days used to typically start at six in the morning and end around midnight in her kitchen, eating her only meal of the day—a bowl of cereal. It was a rare quiet moment at home, for most of her day was spent at a job that she considered unbearable. On paper, the role seemed like a good match for her. She led a startup housed in a large nonprofit, blending her passion for helping others with her entrepreneurial spirit. So what was the problem?

Christina's calendar was a mess! As she started feeling unappreciated at work, she took on side projects. She reasoned that filling her calendar with volunteer work and studying for a second master's degree would make her feel smarter, more talented, and more productive. It didn't. She was exhausted.

Despite a packed schedule, if anyone asked for her time,

she readily gave it to them. It was too easy to say yes to something in the future in order to avoid a difficult or awkward no today. And once an activity was on her schedule, she felt obliged to keep it there. Christina's schedule was completely booked six weeks in advance.

With little time for family or friends, her personal life suffered. She wasn't taking care of her health, stopped dating, and felt crummy. Without a way to organize how she spent her time, she'd let her calendar take over her life.

Christina's first step was to visualize her ideal work life: "I want space to say yes to the spontaneous. I want to be able to be on a delayed train or behind a slow-walking small child and not get frustrated that now I might be late and my tightly controlled day might be entirely thrown off. I want to be less angry."

Next, she exported all her calendar appointments into an Excel spreadsheet, filled in how much time she spent on each activity, then compared that to how she ideally wanted to spend her time. She also rated each activity on how much joy it sparked. She couldn't believe the results. Nearly half her time was spent on activities that didn't bring her joy. She had been making time for the wrong things.

In order to spend time in ways to achieve her ideal work life, Christina stopped automatically saying yes and defaulted to saying no, making exceptions only for activities that mattered most. "I realized that much of that crazy scheduling was because I was adding things that made me happy to make up for all of the things that didn't make me happy, rather than address-ing the things that didn't make me happy," she concluded.

Christina politely canceled any appointment that she didn't think was worthwhile. This included recurring meetings auto-matically added to her calendar, where the organizers usually showed up late and often without an agenda. She also asked others to be conscious of her time, for example, substituting a quick phone call for a thirty-minute appointment. Although a few people were pretty upset by her pushback, most under-stood. She made up a work deadline as an excuse and asked people to reschedule down the road. Only a handful of them followed up to reschedule, which showed that she wasn't the only one who didn't value the meeting.

Of course, Christina still had work responsibilities. She had to answer emails and do other tasks to keep her job, but she was able to eliminate many unneeded activities. With more time on her hands, she started experiencing simple pleasures — making dinner, frequent workouts, monthly brunches, and hanging out with friends on weekends. She soon found the love of her life and became engaged!

As her personal life became active again, an opportunity arose that was made possible only by her new approach to managing her time. She accepted a last-minute invitation to attend a gala. While enjoying her meal, she struck up a conver-sation with an executive at a startup company who soon made her a job offer. This chance encounter provided the opportunity she'd been looking for—a reset of her career and a work environment that appreciated her contributions and valued her time.

All work has its frustrations; Christina's new job was no exception. But she was no longer a slave to a "Say yes to everything" mentality that kept her constantly overscheduled in a job that brought little joy. As she acknowledged, "Not every aspect of my current job brings me joy. However, now I can get a good sense of whether or not I'm looking forward to working on a project. If my collective work doesn't trend toward joy, that's a sign that I need to make a change."

The key to boosting joy at work is to spend more time on activities that bring joy and less time on activities that don't. It sounds simple until our boss hands us an assignment that takes twice as long as he believes it will, a colleague makes a "quick" request, or a client's needs turn our day into a big mess. What can we realistically do to reclaim our time?

Activity Clutter Disrupts Our Days

We can shorten our workdays and add joy to our work if we learn to get ahold of activity clutter. Activity clutter comes from the things we do that take up precious time and sap our energy but don't make a meaningful difference to our personal, professional, or even company's mission. These things include meetings that don't produce new information or better decisions, projects with little chance of being completed, and painstakingly polished presentations that lack substantive content. On average, we spend less than half our workday on our main job responsibilities, with the rest of our time taken up by interruptions, nonessential tasks, administrative tasks, emails, and meetings. How did we end up like this?

Fortunately, psychology provides some answers. There are three traps that can lead to activity clutter: overearning by working too hard for the wrong results, prioritizing urgent tasks over important ones, and multitasking.

The Overearning Trap

I'll be the first to tell you that hard work pays off. When I was a kid, I noticed how parents would boast to others about how smart or talented their children were. Mine never did. Instead, my mother would tell everyone I was a hard worker. It genuinely feels good to accomplish something after trying hard. But what if a lot of your effort goes to waste because you're working toward goals you don't value?

At work, people regularly experience this wasted effort through what psychologists call "overearning." Imagine yourself in one research study. You get invited to a room to listen to pleasant music. It's so relaxing. But you have the chance to give up some of your leisure time to gain some chocolate. By pressing a button to stop the music and replace it with the irritating sound of a saw cutting wood, your relaxation would end but you'd earn a candy. You'd have to eat that candy right after the experiment, so there's no sharing it or saving it for tomorrow.

I love chocolate, and I'd certainly do a little work to earn some. So did most of the research participants. But here's where things went wrong. Once they started earning chocolate, it became difficult for people to stop. By the end of the experiment, participants had worked for far more chocolate than they could physically eat—let alone want to eat.

What this study tells us is that it's all too easy to invest a lot of energy in something that doesn't really matter to us. People lost sight of the fact that their goal was to earn enough chocolate to satisfy themselves and instead tried to maximize the amount that they could earn. Rather than spending their time in a way that earned the reward they wanted, they just kept working until they tired themselves out. And the more people overearned, the less satisfying their chocolate became. They couldn't even enjoy the fruits, or more accurately the chocolate, of their labor!

Earning rewards and being competitive is a part of who we are, but it can derail us easily. When deciding how to spend your time, remember: Don't trade an activity you'd love to pursue for a reward you don't value. Being mindful and aware of what we truly want and who we truly are can protect us from falling into this trap of chasing the wrong goals that we'll later regret.

The Urgency Trap

Instead of making time to dive deeply into our work and experience the joy that can come from tackling an important task, we jump from one seemingly urgent task to the next. That leaves us with very little time to think or grow. Research finds that half of an executive's activities last less than nine minutes, leaving them without much time for deep thought. Factory foremen average 583 discrete activities for an eight-hour shift. Mid-level employees average only one thirty-minute or greater uninterrupted time block about once every other day.

If you're like most, you work on autopilot, accepting and completing assignments based on what appears most urgent, rather than what's actually most important. It's no surprise, then, that more than 50 percent of people feel overwhelmed at least some of the time, which leads to mistakes at work, anger at employers, and resentment toward coworkers.

Guided by psychological quirks that make us think the most urgent activities are also the most important, we often prioritize the wrong ones. Don't confuse urgent and important tasks. They're not the same.

Urgent tasks are those that must be done by a certain time. If not, they can't be done at all — joining a client for dinner on the only day she's in town, helping a colleague meet a project deadline, or attending an annual team retreat.

Important tasks are different. There are big positive outcomes for performing them or big negative consequences for not performing them. Examples include personal development, for instance, through reading and education; updating a product; and developing a good relationship with colleagues.

Some tasks are both important and urgent, and most people prioritize them—whether filing taxes, responding to a job offer, or smoothing things over with an upset customer. Not surprisingly, we usually and correctly deprioritize non-urgent, non-important tasks—whether it's mindlessly checking social media or shopping online during work hours (at least most of the time!).

What about tasks that are urgent but not important, such as attending a weekly company gathering or answering a phone call from a colleague, or that are important but not urgent, such as long-term career planning? Think about it for a minute: What are you likely to work on today? Probably the urgent tasks.

There's a reason why we usually prioritize urgent tasks over important ones. Important tasks tend to be more difficult to complete than urgent ones, making us more reluctant to start them. Urgent tasks have a more immediate payoff, making them more enticing to start and pleasing to finish. If you're trying to feel good—at least in the short term—checking off an urgent task makes sense. In the long term, however, you're not doing the type of work that really matters to your career and company.

We also get tricked into focusing on urgent tasks through artificial deadlines. There's a lot of "fake urgency" at work. After a coworker or client asked you to get back to them within a week, have you ever wondered where the week deadline came from? Too often, it's completely arbitrary. Double-check to make sure a deadline is really the deadline.

And it turns out when we think we're busy with other stuff even if we're not, we're even more prone to being pushed around by fake urgency. With so much to do and now another pressing deadline before us, who has time to figure out which "important" task we should complete first?

The Multitasking Trap

I'm sure you've met people, as I have, who boast of their ability to multitask. They are quick to talk about their superhuman powers that allow them to get everything done—all at once. I used to be very envious of them. I thought about how much time I could save if I could do two things simultaneously. What I didn't realize was that while they were doing many things at once, they usually weren't doing any of them particularly well.

When I became an organizational psychologist, I learned a little secret: despite what we've been led to think, multitaskers tend to be among the least productive people at work.

Research reveals two surprising facts about multitasking: First, it decreases productivity by as much as 40 percent. Second, those who multitask are typically the least capable of doing it successfully.

The human brain can think about only a limited number of things at once. Take on too much, and you'll end up doing a few things poorly rather than any one thing especially well.

Despite what most people believe, multitasking doesn't involve doing several activities simultaneously. It typically means rapidly switching from one task to another without accomplishing any one thing effectively. And since multitaskers don't pay attention to or switch between tasks very well, they make lots of mistakes.

Over time, multitasking leads people to prioritize the wrong activities. Just like those caught in the urgency trap, multitaskers are overly reactive to what's right in front of them at any given moment rather than what is needed for achieving longer-term, and usually more important, goals. As the difficulty of the work increases, the downsides of multitasking increase.

If multitasking makes us less productive, why do people keep doing it? Those who multitask often do so not because they're particularly good at it but because they struggle to block out distractions and focus on a single task. So they compensate by trying to do several things at once. Don't falsely believe that multitaskers are more productive workers and that everyone should aspire to emulate them. Nonsense. Doing many things poorly is not the pathway to productivity.

Make a Task Pile to Find Out What Your Actual Job Is

How do you best use your time when your overloaded calendar pulls you in too many directions at once? The key to escaping the overearning, urgency, and multitasking traps is to be mindful of how you're spending your time—and then shift to activities that spark joy. There's a simple way to hold ourselves accountable for how we spend our days. Instead of asking which activities you should eliminate, ask, *Which ones should I keep?*

Start by putting everything you do in piles. Like the physical items in your workspace that Marie helped you tidy, you'll want to "touch" each of your tasks to feel its gravity and understand its importance. Write each task you regularly do on an index card (or a spreadsheet if you're digitally minded). Research shows that reading on paper makes us more carefully evaluate what's being considered. A physical task pile also serves the same purpose as bringing stuff into a room to see how much you've accumulated. Seeing your own mountain of tasks will help you reflect on what you're doing and why you're doing it.

For most people, you'll probably have three types of task piles: core tasks, project tasks, and developmental tasks.

1. **Core tasks:** These are the central, ongoing activities of your job, the key things you do that justify your existence at work. For a manager in a corporate

environment, core tasks might include budgeting, planning, or leading a facility or team. For a scientist, core tasks might involve designing experiments, analyzing data, and sharing results. For a teacher, core tasks might be designing lessons and grading tests.

2. **Project tasks:** These are the kinds of tasks that have a discrete beginning and end—think planning an event, designing a brochure, or launching a new product.

3. **Developmental tasks:** These are tasks that help us grow or learn, such as training, reading, attending conferences, or taking on a new task. They should advance your work-life vision.

Don't worry if some tasks fall into more than one area. Put these in the most appropriate pile.

What have you discovered about how you spend your time, and how does it relate to your ideal work life? If your ideal work life is to grow, how does the relative size of your developmental task pile stack up against the others? Are you challenging yourself enough? Learning enough? Getting enough feedback from others? If you'd like to connect with others, how many tasks involve working with other people? Are they the people you want to spend time with?

Evaluate Your Tasks to Make Your Job More Joyful

Your task pile is like a mirror—it reflects what you're currently doing. How do you feel when you look in the mirror? I've learned that most people see opportunities to come closer to their ideal work life, but they're not confident enough to make changes. Don't underestimate your control here, or the power that small changes could have on your day-to-day enjoyment of work.

After you've got your tasks in piles, go through each pile, starting with the easiest to tidy (typically your core tasks), followed by project tasks, and concluding with developmental tasks. Pick up each task and ask yourself:

Is this task required for me to keep, and excel, at my job?

Will this task help create a more joyful future, for example, by helping earn a raise, get a promotion, or learn a new skill?

Does this task spark joy and contribute to more satisfaction at work?

Stop doing any task that doesn't meet one of these three conditions.

Now, what if you've got too many tasks that are required but don't spark joy? Or what if your boss won't let you discard any tasks, even the ones you have no reason to keep? Sometimes we're not able to recognize how others benefit from our work. That's a shame, because if we did, work would be a lot more meaningful.

Here's a quick rule I follow: Apply the beneficiary test. Be honest—does anyone read the weekly report you send out, and does it change their decision-making? You can survey your beneficiaries to appraise the usefulness of your work. You might just learn that people do value your work and find new meaning in completing the task.

If you're still convinced the task isn't worth keeping, go talk with your boss. Share the results of your beneficiary test. Your boss might be able to see how your work is important, even if you don't. It's another way for you to learn if there's a hidden impact to your work, which might change your mind about whether the task is worth keeping. After applying the beneficiary test, have an open conversation over the value of the tasks you'd like to discard, and politely remind the boss of the tradeoffs involved in doing them. If all of this fails to convince your boss, maybe your boss is simply unreasonable. But unless you're willing to change jobs, you're just going to have to go along with it. As much as we'd all like to sometimes, we can't toss the boss out!

After you're done, lay out all the remaining tasks so you can look at all of them at once. What do these tasks say about the type of job you have? You might have a title and a job description that portray your job in one way, but the work you do tells a different story. Collectively, do the tasks you kept spark joy or contribute to a more joyful future? If, after tidying, you're still feeling like your tasks are not moving you toward your ideal work life, I've got a few more tips below to make your job better.

If you're satisfied with your pile of tasks, check in periodically to be sure you are continuing to achieve your ideal work life. For any new tasks that come your way, explicitly decide whether they are worth doing before accepting them.

Give Priority to the Activities
That Spark Joy for You

Right now, my work sparks joy, but there was a time when my schedule was so packed, I was physically and mentally exhausted. It was in 2015, just after I was named one of *Time* magazine's 100 Most Influential People, and I was inundated with offers from all over the world.

I accepted as many as I could, seeing them as a great opportunity to share the KonMari Method, but I also happened to be pregnant with my first child, and the pressure took a toll on my mind and body. Sometimes I couldn't control my emotions and would burst into tears at the end of the day.

Finally, I realized that I simply couldn't go on like this. That's when I began changing the way I worked.

My goal in my work is to share the KonMari Method worldwide and help as many people as possible learn to choose joy in their lives through tidying up. But I can't possibly teach others how to spark joy in their lives if I'm not experiencing it in my own.

Since I had that epiphany, I've made it a point to prioritize time for joy in my life, especially when I'm busy. I deliberately schedule in time for things I enjoy or want to do, such as:

* Being with family.
* Brightening up my home with flowers.
* Enjoying a relaxing cup of tea.
* Getting a massage when I'm tired.

These help me to regain my inner balance so that I can return to work refreshed and filled with positive energy. In our busy contemporary world, many of us give priority to our work at the expense of our lives, just as I once did. If that is true for you, my message is this: Make your own physical and emotional well-being top priority.

A jam-packed schedule and work overload lead to burnout. We're not going to be inspired with brilliant ideas or achieve good results when we're totally drained. Even if we love our work, we'll start to hate it and find it hard to keep going.

The first step is to make time to refresh and rejuvenate. Then plan your schedule so that you can work efficiently the rest of the time. In the long run, it's more productive to approach our work with joy and ease of mind.   **M.K.**

Don't Be So Fast to Say Yes

Do you ever feel like your job would be wonderful if people only gave you the space to actually do it? I used to feel that way a lot. As I progressed in my career from an assistant professor fresh out of graduate school to a chaired professor (the highest rank in a university), I was increasingly asked to get involved in activities not central to my core responsibilities of research and teaching, such as serving on lots of committees and attending events. In the spirit of being a good colleague, I almost always said yes. It seemed like the right thing to do, and each activity itself didn't take up a lot of time. But they added up, and they were keeping me from advancing the projects that mattered to me most.

For sure, there are often good reasons to say yes. Some of these activities bring joy, whether from feeling helpful or from the work itself. Some might offer the potential to learn, advance your career, or enjoy social time with colleagues. But some, perhaps too many, simply won't satisfy any of your desires.

I recently came across research that has helped me resist the temptation to constantly say yes. We get lured into agreeing to too many of these types of tasks because we feel guilty saying no. Let go of the guilt. You're already working incredibly hard (look how big your task pile was!). Then try a simple trick: Take a pause.

Given the social pressures to say yes — after all, we want to be seen as good team players — putting off making a decision when approached with these extra requests is one effective technique. Simply say, "I'll think about it and get back to you." Then take some time to decide if the task will spark joy for you. If not, politely decline it. The research shows that when we delay making a commitment, we feel more empowered to say no to tasks we don't enjoy and yes to tasks we do.

Add a Daily Joy

Now that you've stopped doing some activities, you've given yourself room to pick up new tasks that will spark joy. Research shows people make their jobs more satisfying by taking on new responsibilities, volunteering to help out a colleague or even just working on a side project without asking for formal permission. Some bosses will appreciate the initiative. Several companies even have formal policies that allow an employee to spend part of her workweek on a joyful task of her choosing. Of course, if you have a watchful boss and very little freedom about how to do your job, this will be more challenging. But you'll increase your chances of success if you find a way for your daily joy to benefit the business.

Outside of work, give yourself permission for a daily joy, too. For me, I like to read a physical newspaper. I know by the time I start, it's already outdated. But catching up on current events without digital distractions sparks a lot of joy for me.

Create a Clean Space on Your Calendar

It sounds counterintuitive, but to be more productive at work, sometimes you need downtime—a part of your calendar that's a completely clean space. Yes, you heard me right: Research shows that to get more done, you sometimes need to work less. In addition to refreshing your mind, downtime helps you become more creative by giving you time to incubate ideas.

When we're doing seemingly mindless activities such as walking or doodling, we're actually thinking deeply, on a subconscious level. This type of thinking tends to be our most creative because we're not constantly judging ourselves. It can lead to new ways of solving problems and foster innovation. You're still working—and often working smarter—when your calendar isn't jam-packed with tasks. So take a break, feel better, and unlock your imagination!

For my downtime, I walk every day, usually with my phone on airplane mode. A world completely away from any emails, phone calls, or other distractions can let the mind wander. It's also where I feel the freest from self-judgment and allow myself to explore ideas I might otherwise be afraid to head toward.

I know that not everyone has the freedom to walk at or even outside of work. Find something you can do. Most people can close their eyes at their desk and let their mind wander for a couple of minutes. It's a chance to loosen your mind but also a way to show that no matter how confining and out of control your schedule (and job) can sometimes feel, you can take time back—at least for a moment.

———

Tidying your activities will give you a deeper sense of yourself and your true priorities. But it does a lot more than provide a reflection of how you're spending your days. It offers a way to make those days better. By discarding tasks that don't spark joy and adding those that do, you will make your work much more rewarding.

CHAPTER 6

Tidying Decisions

As a single mother, Lisa balanced a full-time position as a high-school art teacher with side jobs as a freelance artist and an online art instructor. Although she loved all her jobs, the number of decisions she regularly made had worn her down. Beyond the major ones relating to her classes—topics to cover, projects to assign, and classroom rules—hundreds, if not thousands, of daily decisions demanded her attention. A day's lesson plan involved countless possibilities: *Will the class work hands-on, watch a video to learn new techniques, or gain graphic skills with the help of a computer?* During class, there were ongoing decisions to be made regarding mentoring students, evaluating them, and even disciplining them. And her side job presented another mountain of decisions: what to make, how to design it, how best to attend to her clients' wishes, and how to build her social media following. *It's just constant decisions about what I'm going to do next,* she thought.

Lisa was finding herself grumpy and exhausted — not just at work but also at home, where she cared for her nine-year-old son. "Decision fatigue is so mentally taxing that I don't remember things ... I have trouble forming my thoughts cohesively and can even forget words."

She knew things had gone from bad to worse when, one Monday morning, she showed up at her high-school class without a lesson plan because she'd put off deciding what to teach until it was too late. *You totally dropped the ball on this, Lisa! You're failing as a teacher!* she scolded herself. She also neglected her budding online teaching business, as her brain was wiped out from the many decisions across her jobs.

Chances are that no matter what type of work you do — whether you're a corporate executive or an entry-level professional — you make thousands of decisions each day. Some researchers estimate that the number is upward of *thirty-five thousand!*

Many decisions are low-stakes ones made with little effort or awareness. We'd be completely overwhelmed if we needed to deliberately think about them — the best path to take when walking to our desk, which pen to use, what to say in a quick email reply. That's why, despite the thousands of decisions we make every day, a recent survey finds that people, on average, recall making only about seventy of them.

Other decisions come with high stakes and require focused attention. We don't face these types of decisions often, but when we do, they rightfully take up a considerable amount of mental and emotional energy. They usually involve the allocation of a relatively large amount of resources. If you're in marketing, these might include deciding the suite of products and services to offer, when and how to rebrand something, and how to position your products in the marketplace; for entrepreneurs, high-stakes decisions could include when to expand and hire employees, whether to raise capital, or whether to sell the business; and for IT professionals, high-stakes decisions involve purchasing major equipment.

Then there are medium-stakes decisions that require much more thought than low-stakes ones and occur much more frequently than high-stakes ones. They're the forgotten or neglected decisions of our work lives. Medium-stakes decisions aren't as easy to make as minor decisions, so we tend to put them off. They're also not as important as high-stakes ones, so they're much easier to forget. That's why Lisa ended up in front of her students without having prepared a lesson plan; it was a medium-stakes decision too difficult to think about the previous day and too easy to forget until she stepped into the classroom.

Generally, medium-stakes decisions focus on delivering or improving your current work tasks, for example, whom to update on a project, how to make a work process better, and how to measure success. If you're a marketing professional, medium-stakes decisions could include what type of market research to gather, when to update the price of a product, and what new forms of advertising to consider and how to measure its effectiveness. If you're an entrepreneur, medium-stakes decisions could include how to improve a product or service and what conferences to attend. And if you're an IT professional, your medium-stakes decisions might include when to upgrade software.

I know that on the surface, tidying decisions appears very different from tidying your physical workspace. Keeping a favorite stapler seems worlds apart from making decisions about how to interact with a customer or when to collaborate with a coworker. But in fact, it's really the same process. Start by asking, *What's worth keeping?* Or, more precisely for this category, *Which decisions deserve my time and energy?*

When considering your many work decisions, follow these simple steps: Forget about the small decisions, sort and organize the medium decisions, and reserve your mental energy for the high-stakes ones.

Most Low-Stakes Decisions Don't Deserve Your Time and Energy

Begin with low-stakes decisions. Keep in mind that what makes something low-stakes is relative to your job and level in the organization. If you're just starting out your career, what might be a low-stakes decision for an executive may have much more significance for you. Chances are that you can't recall many low-stakes decisions, because they're happening automatically and not taking up your brainpower. That's great. Let them keep running on autopilot.

Of those you're conscious of, few are probably worthy of much of your time. Are you:

- picking out a brand of copier paper?
- deciding whether to use a line or bar graph in a presentation?
- choosing a font for your report?

If you don't think the outcome of a decision will make a difference, don't invest a lot of time making it. I know that's hard to do in the moment, and I, too, have been guilty of overthinking things—which hotel to stay at during a work trip, what type of font to use in my classroom handouts, and what type of side dishes to serve to attendees of a conference I'm holding.

It's also possible to automate many low-stakes decisions. Some of my favorites include the following:

- Use services from online retailers to automatically order supplies you need on a regular basis.
- Set decision rules like never scheduling meetings on Friday mornings.
- Create an email signature that automatically fills in "Kind regards," or "Thank you," followed by your name.

You can tailor automating decisions based on your needs and interests. Former Apple CEO Steve Jobs automated his wardrobe—he wore the same type of turtleneck each day. Productivity guru and author Tim Ferriss eats the same breakfast every morning. By not sweating the small decisions, you'll have the time and energy to focus on the more important ones.

Create a Pile of Medium- and High-Stakes Decisions

Gather up all the medium- and high-stakes decisions you currently or will soon face. The high-stakes ones usually pop out, and for most people there will be only a handful of these. Steve Jobs decided to replace the entire board of directors upon returning to Apple and later opted to introduce a phone without a physical keypad, the iPhone. For a middle manager, the high-stakes pile could include how to implement a companywide change and whom to hire to the team. And for new professionals, selecting a trusted mentor is likely a high-stakes decision.

Medium-stakes decisions are what's left in the middle. For most people, you can identify your own medium-stakes decisions by considering which ones will notably make your work better, for example, decisions about improving processes, updating products or services, getting advice on problems, and communicating progress to others.

Briefly summarize each medium- and high-stakes decision on an index card (as with tidying time, you can also use a spreadsheet). Most people will have a manageable number of decisions, no more than twenty.

Sort Through Your Decision Pile

After you've put all your decisions in a pile, write an "H" next to each high-stakes decision. These are decisions that will have a big impact on your work or life and deserve your time and energy. Keep all of them and put them to the side.

You're now left with the medium-stakes decisions, and it's time to figure out which ones are truly worth keeping. Pick up each index card and follow a simple rule: **If making the decision is critical for the work you do, if it will help you advance your work-life vision, or if it sparks joy, keep it.**

Now figure out what to do with the decisions you kept. As you're holding each decision, ask yourself:

Is there another person who will be affected more by the decision and who should make it?

Who has the best judgment and information to make the decision?

Can I entrust someone else to make the decision?

How frequently does the decision need to be made? Can it be automated and checked on only periodically?

If it feels like someone else should make the decision, delegate it, if possible (mark the index card with a "D" and write the name of whom you'd like to assign it to). It's sometimes difficult, but not impossible, to delegate to someone at the same rank as you or higher. Asking politely and providing a reasonable explanation for why the person is better suited for the decision goes a long way. And offering to take responsibility for one of their decisions in return strengthens your case. Just make sure it's one worth making.

If the decision doesn't need yours or anyone else's regular involvement, automate it (mark the index card with an "A" along with a time to implement automation).

As you face new decisions, you'll have the experience and

confidence to tidy those, too. Keep focusing on the high-stakes decisions and the most valuable medium-stakes ones. Be choosy about what you spend your time and energy on. You might realize that what you previously viewed as an important decision either shouldn't be made or should be made by someone else. Part of being a good decision maker is realizing when it's time not to be involved!

————

After learning about Lisa's struggles, we found ways to help her tidy her decisions. As with a large pile of clothing, putting all her high-stakes and medium-stakes decisions in one place helped Lisa understand the magnitude of her problem. She was constantly feeling overwhelmed because she had too many decisions to make.

The following week, she looked at her decision pile and realized that she made some decisions over and over again, particularly those that involved managing her high-school students' classroom behavior and answering questions on her freelance business's Instagram account.

Lisa was able to eliminate 9 percent of the decisions in her pile and either automate or delegate 40 percent of them. For instance, she now starts every day with the same activity. Students work on the previous day's project, freeing her up to take attendance without interruption. She also has students take a more active role in evaluating their own work, which has reduced the number of decisions she needs to make.

Lisa also opted to post to her business's Instagram account every morning and then respond to comments twice a day.

After clearing out her decision clutter, the remaining decisions mostly required high degrees of creativity—what kind of art to create, what bigger-picture business decisions she needed to make, and what courses to design for her online business. These were the types of decisions that sparked joy for her.

When I followed up with Lisa, the results of her tidying were abundantly clear. "I have a renewed sense of things actually being possible...I can't believe how much clarity this has created for me." She found the time, motivation, and skill to make one very high-stakes decision: She opted to quit her teaching profession and focus on her own business. Soon her business income nearly tripled. But the biggest change came from her newfound love of her work and life. "This process is the beginning of something really huge for me," she wrote to me. "I'm still finding myself feeling so much joy...My creative juices really took off!!! I don't think it would've happened if I hadn't tidied my decisions...I'm so much more productive and happy." And it went beyond her work. Lisa's relationship with her son dramatically improved, she lost fifteen pounds within a month of tidying her decisions, and she gained a rekindled sense of optimism.

Tidying Choices: More Options Aren't Always Better

Let's now look at how we actually make decisions. It's pretty reasonable to think that the more choice we have, the better off we are. If you're evaluating a supplier or vendor, the more companies to look at, the better. If you're deciding on investments for your retirement plan, the more mutual funds to pick from, the better. If you're trying to take the best job, you'd want as many options as possible.

It's true that having more choices can be a good thing, but only up to a point. For some decisions, people can become overloaded with so many possibilities that they make poorer decisions and are less satisfied with whatever they ultimately do pick. How about the options we passed up: the job we didn't take, the project we managed one way versus another, a market we could have entered versus the one we did, or the mentor we didn't pick? Our minds are incredibly persuasive at convincing us that no matter what path we took, we could've made a better choice.

For most decisions, it's a lot of work to consider more than five picks. When someone needs you to make a decision, ask that they offer at most five options. If you're on your own, solicit advice from colleagues to narrow down your choices to the top prospects and then make your decision. This will help reduce the regret of not considering an option.

Research points to a few other simple ways to tidy choices.

First, if the choices are very similar, realize there's probably more than one good choice, so just pick one. Second, put your choices in a commonsense order, for example, from most expensive to least expensive or from biggest risk/reward to lowest risk/reward. Third, sifting through a lot of choices is tiresome if you're trying to figure out what you want at the same time. Imagine searching for a new job. If you know beforehand that you'd like a high-growth opportunity, a short commute, and a lot of freedom, having a bigger set of potential jobs to pick from can be helpful. You would best match your desires (growth, commute, and freedom) with the available jobs. However, if you're unsure of your preferences, more choices can be overwhelming.

Good Enough Is Good Enough for Most Decisions

I want you to give up on the idea of needing to always make a perfect decision. Sometimes you will, but many times you won't. That might be hard to swallow, but here's why it's okay: In most cases, a good-enough decision will be good enough. Striving for perfection is often unnecessary and comes at a cost. It both wastes time that can be better spent on other activities and creates feelings of frustration and disappointment when you didn't make the perfect choice.

Before making a decision, ask what type of outcome will spark joy for you. There's no use in seeking a perfect decision when a good-enough one will make you just as happy. Plus, with so much changing in the world, any decision you make might be temporary. If you spend too much effort seeking a perfect solution, you'll likely be overly committed to that solution, even if it's no longer working. That's why good enough is often more than good enough.

To avoid perfectionist tendencies, set a deadline for your decision-making. The gain from excessive thought and discussion won't be worth the time and effort invested. Be flexible about updating your decision if new information emerges. And remember, for most decisions, the consequences are not as high as you might think.

———

When you tidy your decisions, you focus on what really makes an impact. You then sort through what's worth your time and energy, and what should be eliminated, delegated, or automated. Your decisions are freed from the clutter of an overwhelming number of choices, and you connect to what you're trying to accomplish. Difficult decisions suddenly feel easier to make. When it comes to the important decisions that demand your time and energy, you'll be more engaged and satisfied no matter what you pick.

CHAPTER 7

Tidying Your Network

nstagram is an important social media platform for artists, and Lianne, a British painter and illustrator, had an impressive fifteen thousand followers. As exciting as it seemed, staying connected with so many followers took its toll. So many unimportant messages made it hard to respond to the truly important ones: interested buyers. She also had her fair share of trolls. People would make rude comments, sometimes dumb and other times borderline abusive. As these mounted, she found that she was increasingly drained by the time-consuming and emotionally exhausting aspects of her network.

Lianne spent so much time on social media that she neglected her work and life. "I'm a mother and I'm an artist," she proudly told me. "I don't have time to waste tweeting ten times a day." The truth is, however, Lianne was spending more time on Instagram than on her actual art.

She decided to do something courageous.

Lianne deleted her Instagram account, dropping all her followers. "In today's society, people want more and more followers, but that's not my goal," she reasoned. A large network was doing little to help her sell her art. "When you're trying to sell something like art, I'd much prefer to have fifty passionate followers who buy art over fifteen thousand vaguely interested followers who send me rude messages." Restarting with zero followers allowed her to be more selective and connect only with people who actually appreciated her work.

It's easy to think of networking, whether in person or online, as an exercise in gaining as many connections as possible: phone contacts, Facebook friends, Instagram followers, LinkedIn ties, or Twitter followers. Readily trackable metrics make us feel good as the numbers grow. We can compare our figures with those of our colleagues and friends, mistakenly believing that more connections make us more important. Or more popular. Or more successful. Let me tell you something: Having a large network means only one thing—that you've accumulated a large network!

Make your network a source of joy. Build one full of people whom you enjoy spending time with and helping, who care about your development and success, and with whom you're comfortable revealing your setbacks and seeking their counsel.

How Big a Network Do You Need?

With a large network, the chances increase that someone might know something that could help you, such as an unadvertised job opportunity or the answer to a difficult question. That's the logic that drives people to invest so much time growing their network. People you're already close to—both at work and socially—are already sharing what they know with you. But most of the contacts in a large network are people with whom you seldom interact, so there's more you can learn from them. There's a big difference, though, between having a network full of valuable contacts and having a network full of valuable contacts *truly willing to help.*

Karen, a startup investor and former tech executive, first tried the typical path to networking, meeting as many people as she could. "I probably spent the better part of a year going to conferences and meeting a lot of people," she told me. "Looking back, those weren't the most genuine experiences and connections. It was a numbers game." It was exhausting and, ultimately, a waste of time.

After reflecting on networking events that always seemed to disappoint her, she vowed to make a change. Karen stopped trying to cast such a wide net and instead shifted to forming deeper bonds with a smaller number of people. That approach quickly got put to the test when she was evaluating a potential investment in a company and had a technical set of research she promptly needed. While modest in size, her network included one woman who she thought might be able to help. Karen reached out to her and within hours had a detailed response. "The research would have taken me weeks to complete," Karen explained. Because Karen had already forged a strong relationship with her contact, she got the help she needed almost immediately. A few days later, she sent the contact who had come through for her a handwritten thank-you note.

Karen has reaped other benefits from her slimmed-down approach. "I'm way less anxious about going to networking events.... It's freed up a lot of cognitive space," she says.

Large networks also make it difficult to form meaningful connections. Studies conclude that people can reasonably handle about 150 meaningful connections. Beyond that, it's hard to genuinely know people in your network. Try a simple exercise. When you think about all your contacts and friends, can you picture the faces of everyone in your network? Do they all spark joy? Probably not.

Even for those with large networks, most of their interactions come from a small subset of their networks. Many of the "friends" in our network have little interest in sincerely connecting with us, and instead call on us only when they need a favor. Christina, who learned to tidy her time in chapter 5, found this out the hard way. As a Harvard MBA alumna, she thought she'd reap many benefits from the big, prestigious network. Over time, she realized that this network produced few meaningful connections but lots of requests. "I reached a point where in a two-week period, I had ten different people emailing me asking to pick my brain," she explained. "These weren't friends or people who had invested in a relationship with me in any way." Her willingness to honor these requests took a toll on her career and life, leaving her feeling burned out.

Growing your network is not only time-consuming but, when it comes to online networking, potentially harmful to your psychological well-being. Research has shown that the more time we spend on social media, the less happy we are. That's because people usually share only good news on social media, while very few use it to share bad news. How many LinkedIn notifications have you received that said, "I've just been fired!" or "I screwed up big-time at work today." Stop comparing yourself with someone's persona on social media and instead ask what progress you're making toward your ideal work life. That's the only comparison that matters.

Marie's Approach to Tidying Networks

One of the most important points in building a joyful network is knowing what kind of connections you enjoy. For example, some people love being surrounded by friends and having fun together. Others prefer to have deeper relationships with just a few people. I fall into the latter category. I'm not very good at keeping in touch, and I feel more comfortable with fewer relationships.

But when I quit the company and started to work as an independent consultant, I poured my efforts into making connections with as many people as possible because I wanted to introduce my business. I joined seminars and gatherings for people from different fields, exchanging many business cards. Gradually, however, I noticed something wasn't quite right.

The more people I knew, the more invitations I received to events and parties, and the more packed my schedule became. I no longer had time to do what I really wanted. I was so swamped with emails that I struggled to respond to them all. When I looked at the names in my notebook, the number of people whose faces I couldn't remember kept increasing.

It didn't feel good to be inundated with information, and I wondered if it wasn't rather dishonest to stay connected with people I couldn't even remember. The more my connections increased, the more uncomfortable I felt, so I decided to reset my network.

Using the KonMari Method, I looked at each name and kept only those that sparked joy. The number of names in my address book and my apps dropped drastically, and in the end I was left with only ten people, excluding my family and people whose contacts were essential for work. To be honest, I was stunned at how many names I eliminated, but afterward my heart felt much lighter, and I was better able to nurture those relationships that I had chosen to keep.

Because I now had more time and mental space, I contacted my family more often and could thank my friends sincerely, even for little things. I also felt far more gratitude than before for these precious people with whom I had decided to stay in touch.

Since I reset my network, I've made it a habit to periodically review my relationships and to be thankful for them. I write down the names of all the people with whom I am currently involved and jot down my feelings of gratitude. This makes me value them even more and helps me nurture warmer relations. This practice is perfect for me because, when I'm busy and engrossed in my work, I tend to forget to be considerate of the people around me.

Just as you would to create a joyful lifestyle, choose what sparks joy and take care of what you decide to keep—you need to do both of these things to build a joyful network. When you feel something's not quite right with your network, see that as a sign. Believe that you can have a more fulfilling life and contribute more to the lives of others when you are comfortable. Then say goodbye with gratitude to any relationships you no longer need and nurture those that you decide to keep.   **M.K.**

Evaluate Your Contacts to Identify Joy-Sparking Relationships

You probably have connections in many places: LinkedIn, Facebook, and other social networks along with the contacts lists on your smartphone and email platform. And Marie has already helped you tidy your business cards. It's probably going to be very time-consuming to get your different contacts lists into a single, integrated pile. For relationships, it's okay to tidy platform by platform. Clean up contacts for all these platforms in a similar way. Start by imagining your ideal work life. Who are the people and what kinds of people do you want to be surrounded by and spend your time with?

Think about each person and ask yourself: *Which connections do I need for my job?* Connecting to colleagues or business partners is sometimes part of the job.

Next, ask yourself: *Which connections can help me*

advance my work-life vision? These connections help bring about a joy-sparking future, such as a new (and better) job or opportunities to gain valuable information or insight, such as sales leads or helpful advice.

Finally, ask yourself: *Which connections bring me joy?* For example, *Do I smile when I think of this person? Would I be happy to see them soon?* Some might bring joy because you have meaningful relationships with them. Others might be people you enjoy spending time with or helping or mentoring.

If a person doesn't fit into one of the three groups above, delete them from your contacts, stop following them, or mute their social media feed. Many social media platforms allow you to drop connections or at least stop receiving notifications from them without their knowledge.

In the future, give yourself permission to be choosy about your connections. I used to impulsively respond yes to every LinkedIn or Facebook friend request because of the short-term high I'd get from adding yet another contact. But I realized that I wasn't really building a network but rather just accumulating a bunch of loose associations. And don't feel obligated to accept every in-person meeting request or attend every networking event in your area. This may sound harsh, but it will free you up to be present for and invested in the connections that matter most.

How to Make High-Quality Connections

Tony, whom we first met in chapter 4, recently celebrated his third promotion in seven years. As a sales and marketing professional in the energy industry, you might think that Tony had built up a formidable network to support his fast-track career. Not so.

After a major restructuring at his company, his supervisor was let go and Tony thought that he, too, might soon suffer the same fate. Instead of reaching out to a wide group of contacts, he talked to four people with whom he already had quality relationships. He immediately found four promising opportunities. "It wasn't about the quantity of my contacts. I didn't have thirty people to call. I only had a few, but they were all high-quality people," he says.

When you have a limited network, it's critical to make sure you're building the right connections. Research finds that high-quality connections involve two people who genuinely care for each other, even when facing tough times such as a tight deadline, a bad mistake, or, in Tony's case, a threat to his career. We share our true feelings with these people, we learn from them, and the relationships we forge are able to withstand setbacks.

My mentor, Jane, is not only a renowned expert on high-quality connections but also an exemplar of how to build them in our professional lives. While working at the University of Michigan, she showed that quality connections with colleagues can contribute to lots of positive outcomes, including better physical and psychological health, learning, and creativity.

To build high-quality connections, first you must be present. Adding a quick Facebook "like" of a friend's post or passing along a pre-filled "Congratulations" when someone broadcasts a promotion on LinkedIn is easy but so obviously meaningless. Don't ask "How are you?" if you're not prepared for a five-minute answer that might not be entirely enjoyable. And don't answer with a shallow "Good" if you'd like to build a high-quality connection. I remember the first time Jane asked me how I was doing. I quickly answered "Good," assuming she was just being polite. I can still vividly picture her reaction, looking me straight in the eye and asking more firmly, "No, how are you really doing?" She wouldn't accept my first answer because it wasn't going to foster a real friendship. She needed to imagine herself in my shoes so she could truly learn about what was going on in my life. And I had to get over my fear of making myself vulnerable by confiding in someone whose esteem and respect I wanted (and needed). Even though she was an eminent scholar (and I was a student), she was still a person who desired a genuine connection.

Second, help others do their best work. When people realize that you genuinely want to help them, they open up to forming a high-quality connection. Mentorship is a great way to achieve this, but it's not the only way. Less formal ways of assisting others include simply lending a hand to a coworker in need or volunteering to listen. We can make a big difference in others' lives by being a sounding board, offering to share constructive feedback on a project, or advocating for their projects. Jane has dedicated so much of her career to helping students in ways few mentors do. And the results speak for themselves, as she has trained some of the most influential professionals in her field.

Third, be open and trust others. Make yourself even more vulnerable — letting people know about your mistakes and being upfront about your shortcomings. You make yourself approachable and show that you, too, are able to grow. That's hard to do when you're so busy being insecure about your own standing at work. And if you're a leader, others sometimes put you on a pedestal, which makes it that much harder to reach you. Even the most talented and amazing person you work with makes lots of mistakes — just like you! Stop pretending you're perfect. It will allow you to start connecting in more meaningful ways.

Another way of building trust is to authentically delegate. Don't assign someone work and then constantly monitor their progress and ignore their ideas. Even when I was a brand-new PhD student, Jane trusted me to work on important parts of research projects. And when I messed up, she was quick to point out the many times she too had screwed up and acknowledge it as part of any project.

Fourth, encourage play. Not only does it provide a release

to sometimes be silly but it also deepens our thinking and ignites our creativity. Team or companywide events that celebrate an achievement can encourage fun, but the more spontaneous and self-organized events usually are more authentic and feel less forced.

In her career, Jane has organized many events involving prominent international scholars. Professors tend to be a pretty introverted, serious, and cynical bunch. Yet she always finds a way to get them to play. One of her favorite ways is to hand out a conference item that symbolizes the event's theme while also encouraging everyone to get in a lighthearted mood—for example, plant seeds for a conference on professional growth.

———

Instead of blindly saying yes to every request for mentorship, advice, or other kinds of help, build relationships that matter the most. It's perfectly fine to say no to superficial requests, just as it's personally rewarding to use your network to help people you really care about. Let's replace networking with high-quality connecting, substituting large networks that often have little substance with smaller networks of connections that truly spark joy.

CHAPTER 8

Tidying Meetings

Gavino had spent much of his career in the public sector, serving in law enforcement and later in the United States Army. It was a satisfying career, with highlights including updating the curriculum and operations of a police academy and helping secure free elections in Afghanistan. But it was also one full of meetings. With required daily briefings, Gavino found himself in meetings even when there was nothing to discuss.

Eventually Gavino left public service to work for a global consulting firm. He helps some of the largest companies in the world put their human resource functions, such as payroll and vacation tracking, onto a single technology platform.

The corporate world, Gavino quickly discovered, is very different from his public sector employers. Without regimented protocols, leaders could determine when, and how, to conduct their meetings.

His first project was for a Florida-based manufacturer. The project's co-leaders had similar backgrounds and positions in the consulting company. Although both co-leaders attended each other's meetings, when the leadership baton passed from one to the other, the meetings ran differently. John, the first leader, preferred to schedule frequent, painstakingly long meetings. Mark scheduled fewer meetings that were shorter and more succinct.

Discussions in John's meetings were aimless, ending only when everyone became so tired, they just stopped talking. At one drawn-out meeting among his consulting colleagues, someone hatched a plan to set them free: make a run for the bathroom. After one woman asked to use the restroom, others immediately followed her, finally ending the meeting. "These meetings literally take you from your work and make your day that much longer... it's almost seen as punishment... it kills your enjoyment of work," Gavino grumbled.

Mark's meetings, on the other hand, started on time and often ended early, thanks to a preset agenda. Gavino felt motivated and engaged during and after these meetings, ready to put in his best effort and make a valuable contribution.

As much as meetings let us down, we need them. They're where we come up with new ideas, make significant decisions, learn from others, and work together. According to one study, more than 15 percent of a person's satisfaction with their job is based on satisfaction with the meetings they attend. That's a pretty high number when you consider the many factors that influence job satisfaction, such as the type of work one does, pay, promotion opportunities, and your relationship with the boss.

When we lead and participate in well-run meetings, it's much easier to experience joy at work. Yet there's no doubt that when led poorly, meetings become a major pain point and one of the greatest obstacles to our productivity. They decrease our engagement, emotionally exhaust us, and sap the joy from work. But as Gavino's experience illustrates, meetings aren't necessarily the problem. It's possible to be more productive with fewer and shorter meetings. No matter your title or role, there are simple steps that you can take to help make meetings twice as effective in half the time while adding a refreshing element of joy!

Imagine Your Ideal Meeting

Before you start to tidy your meetings, think about what an "ideal meeting" looks like—both the meetings you attend and any you might formally lead. Even if you're just starting your career and find yourself at the mercy of how others lead meetings, it's important that you know what you want to get out of meetings. If you tell yourself that every meeting you attend is going to be a downer, that's what's going to happen.

Would you describe your ideal meeting as one that has a clear purpose and goal? Active participation? People listening to one another, respecting one another's opinion, and having fun? A meeting where you're able to show results in a short amount of time?

Write down or think about how you'd like an ideal meeting to feel and what outcomes it would produce.

Gather Your Meetings

You might not realize how much of your time and effort go into meetings because they're scattered throughout the week. It's time to gather all your meetings in one place.

Go through your calendar for the past week and identify all the meetings you attended. Be sure to include any that weren't formally scheduled, such as a last-minute huddle. Now, using an index card for each meeting (or a spreadsheet, as before), write its name, the number of minutes you spent in it, and the frequency you attend.

Next, pick up each card and ask yourself:

Was it required for my job? For example, did it offer information that you couldn't have learned from reading something? Did it help solve critical problems? Did it result in making a key decision or plan of action? Did you need to show up because the boss would be angry if you didn't? For weekly meetings, is going each time really necessary?

Did it help move me closer to my ideal work life? For example, did you learn something to advance your career?

Did it bring joy? For example, did it make you feel more connected to your colleagues? Did you have fun?

Rip up the index card of any meeting that doesn't satisfy at least one of these conditions. Remember to say thank you for what it taught you (even if it taught you how not to run a meeting!).

For those meetings that you're responsible for organizing, go through each index card with the mindset that you're going to cancel all the ones you've already arranged. Nothing is sacred—the weekly touch-base, the quarterly offsite, the end-of-semester debrief, or the bimonthly project meeting. Keep only recurring meetings that regularly result in the best work and bring the greatest satisfaction to participants—until they're no longer needed or useful. Just because they brought great results in the past doesn't mean they should continue forever.

Now put the remaining index cards in front of you so you can look at them all at once. What do they tell you about your job? Are you spending too much time in meetings and not enough doing your job? Are most of the meetings requirements for the job, and too few are bringing you closer to your ideal work life? Are you finding your days occupied by attending meetings only to please the boss?

Separate Messy Meetings from Irrelevant Ones

Do your best to get excused from any meeting that's not necessary, isn't helpful for realizing a joyful future, or doesn't spark
joy. The truth is that even with our best efforts, this isn't going to
be possible all the time. For some people, given the nature of
where they work, it might never be doable. You'll need to use
your judgment about your own working conditions. But many
people have more latitude than they realize.

There are two reasons people usually don't want to attend
any given meeting: because it's disorganized or because it's not
particularly relevant to their work. I'll explain later how anyone
can help organize a meeting better. Tidying can improve these
meetings, and because they're relevant, they are worth keeping. You can work to help them reach their full potential.

If you find a meeting's purpose not relevant for learning or
contributing, it's time to try to stop going. Your attendance is
not advancing your ideal work life or serving another purpose,
such as helping colleagues with their work. Tony, the marketing
professional in the energy industry whom we first met in chapter 4, now considers the potential value in each meeting before
attending. Many of his colleagues work late into the evening
because they're shuffling from meeting to meeting all day and
never have a chance to complete their project work. "Probably
only 10 percent of the meetings are worth their time," he
estimates.

Tony takes a direct approach. He's learned that being a good team player grants him some degree of leeway to politely decline meetings. Although he's a mid-level employee who doesn't arrange the meetings, he's developed the judgment to know which ones are worth attending. And he isn't bashful about telling his boss when he feels it would not be useful for him to go. "If I go to this meeting, it will detract from work that actually adds value to our shareholders," he likes to say.

Many companies value meetings so highly that it's not realistic to skip them without taking additional steps. Some people might not have the confidence or standing to explicitly opt out of meetings. You might feel compelled to attend because it's intimidating, and perhaps even unwise, to tell a colleague that you're not coming to a meeting. Imagine how that conversation would go. "I'm sorry, but your meeting exhausts me and it's pointless. I'm going to skip it." And when your boss calls the meeting, it feels impossible to say no. So what can you do?

Consider requesting a description of the meeting's broad purpose and an agenda beforehand. Do it out of a genuine desire to come prepared. You might just realize the meeting is relevant to your work. But if you still have doubts about what you can learn or contribute, follow up with simple questions. Frame them in ways that show you are interested in wanting to have a successful meeting so the organizer won't feel defensive. Ask questions such as: *How can I best contribute to the success of this meeting? How can I best prepare for this meeting?* These give you a quick, low-risk way to get a sharper sense of your role during a meeting. They may even help the organizer conclude that your presence isn't necessary.

If, after this preliminary effort, you're still convinced that you don't have anything to add, politely ask to be excused. You can let the organizer know that you're not the right person to attend. Research shows that providing an explanation, such as not having relevant information or a stake in the outcome, will boost your chances. If you can, nominate a person who can make a more valuable contribution to the meeting.

If all else fails and you're stuck in that dreadful meeting, identify at least one thing you can learn from it.

Going to More Meetings Doesn't Make You More Valuable

Be honest with yourself about whether you're inadvertently contributing to your big meeting pile. When I ask people if their schedule is filled with too many meetings, they'll almost always say yes. But when I ask them how they'd feel if they didn't get invited to a meeting, they're just as likely to take it as a personal insult or a sign of marginalization. Try to get rid of the thought that the more meetings you attend, the more important you are. Do you really need to or even want to attend? Are you just trying to participate because it feels like it will signal your value?

Or are you worried about missing out on an important conversation or key decision? Remember, meetings are just one of many ways you can make a difference. Your goal is not to win the award for most meetings attended.

Anyone Can Bring More Joy to a Meeting

When you step into a meeting, you're entering a shared space for collaboration, decision-making, and exchanging ideas. Treasure this space, and it will turn into a source of joy. Don't use it to advance your narrow self-interests. Meetings are not the place to make long-winded speeches, come in with a closed mind, or put down colleagues' ideas in order to promote your own.

Rule #1: Show up. Really show up. I've observed far too many meetings where few people are truly present and engaged. Sit up straight, pull yourself close to the table, and radiate positive energy. This is not the time to let your mind wander.

Rule #2: Come prepared. If a leader provided an agenda beforehand, make sure you're ready. If you feel like you don't have enough time to prepare yourself, you probably don't have time to attend the meeting, either. Ask yourself again: *Was this meeting really worth keeping?*

Rule #3: Put away your electronics. Seriously, we all see you sneaking a peek at your phone. It's rude and sends the message that the meeting is unimportant and unworthy of your attention. It clutters the room with lots of noises, from notifications to tapping on the screen. Once one person does it, others will follow, and the group will treat the meeting without the respect it deserves. If you focus on the meeting, it will be shorter, more effective, and more enjoyable.

Rule #4: Listen . . . *really* listen! We should be able to learn from one another during meetings. That's pretty hard to do, because we all enjoy talking. In one set of experiments, researchers found that people wanted to talk so much that they were willing to give up earning some cash to talk even more. A look at people's brain imaging during the study revealed that talking provides the same feelings of satisfaction as eating or having sex. It's no wonder, then, that meetings quickly become cluttered with lots of talking that doesn't stay on topic — and too little listening.

Rule #5: Speak up. There are times when you have unique information to share. Focus on advancing the conversation with new information, a different perspective, or putting the discussion back on track. If you find that the group needs more critical thinking, ask to play the "devil's advocate" or to represent a "competitor" or other stakeholder, such as another group in the company, a regulator, or a customer. Although an effective leader will cut off redundant and unhelpful discussions, a good meeting participant can regulate his or her own behavior and realize when it's time to speak up and when it's time to listen based on a simple rule: *Am I offering new information that advances a goal of the meeting?* If not, it's time to listen to others.

Rule #6: Do no harm. We're responsible adults. Blaming others, cutting them off, or self-promoting creates dysfunction. In one remarkable study of ninety-two team meetings, bad meeting behavior did much more harm to a meeting than positive behaviors did good. So, at the very least, leave your snide remarks and bad attitude at your desk.

Finally, support others. Instead of immediately rejecting what a person says, try improving upon it. Replace a "No, but" with a "Yes, and" to abolish your instinct to reject others' ideas and condition yourself to build on them. They will feel better—and you will, too, for helping them.

Run a Tidy Meeting

Maybe you're a manager who regularly leads meetings. Or perhaps you aspire to move up in your career and take on additional responsibilities, which likely will include facilitating meetings. You might work with clients and need to organize your discussions with them to get better results. Possibly, your boss might come to you one day and ask you to run a meeting in her absence. Will you be ready? No matter your position, learning to run a tidy meeting is a skill that will serve you well.

First, know what you want to accomplish. Is a meeting even

necessary? Some meetings are purely informational, and usually there's a more efficient way to share this information. A simple handout or a few slides might capture what you're going to cover. Let people quickly get the update on their own time and reserve meetings for discussions and decision-making.

With automated recurring meetings, the default is for the weekly meeting to go on unless someone actively cancels it. Can you instead replace a recurring meeting with an occasional one when you've got something important to cover?

Second, think carefully about the participants. Given digital scheduling, it's too easy to invite others to join. It's also tempting to add as many people as possible, either to make the meeting seem more important or because you think it will run more smoothly. If you were going to write them a handwritten invitation, would you take the time to include them?

The reality is that too many people slow down a meeting. What's more important than having a full room is having the *right* people in the room—those who have unique information to contribute or authority to take action or make a decision.

Third, state the goals of the meeting in the invitation. That will help people decide if they're truly needed. If they're not, give them permission to skip it without consequences. If you find that the meeting isn't as effective without a particular person present, let them know the difference their participation would make. If the meeting moves along fine without them, they weren't really needed.

Make sure the agenda contains enough details so that people can adequately prepare. For example, you can identify the specific decisions or proposed actions to debate, ask people to think about questions beforehand, and invite them to come with specific ideas.

Fourth, encourage participation. You invited people to make contributions, and there's no faster way to demoralize a group of people than to keep talking yourself. Make it clear from the very start that your goal is to bring out everyone's ideas — and not have everyone just listen to you or agree with everything you say. When leaders talk too much, it slows down decision-making, lowers productivity, and leads to worse decisions overall.

Avoid going around the table and asking each person to say something. Instead, ask everyone to jump in when they have anything new to add. Invite their active involvement with open-ended questions that foster debate and make it safe for everybody to speak freely. You can ask questions such as: What's another way to look at this problem? What blind spots should we look out for? How will our customers, employees, or other constituents feel?

If people are not participating, especially at a recurring meeting, have a quick conversation with them to encourage their input the next time. Do they feel they don't have anything to add? If so, is that because they're not the best person to attend? Excuse them. If they lack confidence, for instance, if they're the lowest-ranked person at the meeting, let them know that you invited them because you want their opinion.

Fifth, set timelines for meetings. Thirty and sixty minutes are common because they're round numbers, but other than that, there's really no logic to them. Meetings rarely end early, even if the work is finished. If they're scheduled for several hours, they'll go on for several hours.

Once your meetings pass sixty minutes, people are likely checking out. With too much time, the first half of meetings tends to be unproductive, as there is a lack of urgency. Beyond taking up less time, a shorter meeting and moderate amount of time pressure can spark creativity.

Try reducing existing meetings by fifteen-minute increments until you find that you're too short on time.

Although overly long meetings sap our energy, be careful not to replace them with more frequent, short meetings. Most people readily say yes to short-meeting requests, but short meetings can be almost as costly as long ones (and that's assuming they stay short, which rarely happens!). Preparing for them is time-consuming, and they disrupt our other work. In one study, researchers found that minutes spent in meetings had little impact on employees' well-being. What mattered was the number of meetings they attended. The constant disruptions that come from many short meetings left them feeling far more dispirited and exhausted than from a few longer ones. They also found that having more meetings didn't increase productivity. It's much better to bundle a bunch of related issues into one meeting of around forty-five minutes than to schedule several short meetings throughout the week.

Hold "standing" meetings, without a traditional conference table and chairs, as they lead to more creative ideas and more collaboration. Sitting symbolically marks territory, which leads people to become overly possessive about their own ideas and less open to new ones. In contrast, standing makes people more engaged and less territorial. An added bonus is that standing meetings tend to be shorter.

Finally, just as a meeting needs a purpose and an agenda, it also needs a recap. Start off by thanking everyone for participating. People took time out from their busy schedules to support the agenda, so you owe them a sincere expression of gratitude. A recap should help them understand why their time was well spent. Ask questions such as: What progress did we make? What got in the way? What did we learn? What did we solve? At the end of a meeting where something is decided, ask people to publicly commit to working to support it, even if they weren't in favor of the decision. With this public declaration, they're much more likely to follow through, and less likely to engage in back-channel after-discussions with others in which they undermine or sabotage the decision.

———

Imagine meetings that are energizing—and ones you actually look forward to attending. They make progress on prized projects and sometimes even end early. This vision is within your reach if you do your part to tidy meetings. Help everyone start experiencing more joy in the conference room!

CHAPTER 9

Tidying Teams

Marcos landed his dream job. As a senior sourcing analyst overseeing IT purchases for all of North America for a major energy company, Marcos was excited to go to work every day. But a year into his job, the energy industry plunged. His position was eliminated. Marcos's manager gave him an ultimatum: leave the company or move to a new team.

Marcos was understandably upset. He didn't want to leave his old team, and the work on the new one sounded pretty boring—sifting through and fixing the fifteen thousand bills the company received each month. Not wanting to be out of work, he reluctantly joined the new team and started the mind-numbing task of correcting billing errors. "It was painful. I was hurt," he reflected.

Upon arriving, he realized the team's work was a complete

mess. With a double-digit error rate, too many invoices went unpaid or incorrectly paid. The fifteen-person team also had no formal leader. Marcos stepped up. *You've been given the worst job in the supply-chain organization,* he told himself. *Can you become a leader without a title?* He became the go-to guy to fix invoice mistakes, helping to make other people's jobs easier. The guidance he provided to the rest of the team made his efforts all the more impactful.

His efforts made a big difference. The team gelled, people started actually liking their jobs, and the group cut the error rate by a few percentage points. They were getting noticed for their quality work. Soon enough, management rewarded Marcos with a new position in supply-chain analytics, a more respected part of the company. When he left the invoice group, management offered his successor the formal position of team leader, a recognition Marcos never received, but a testament to the impact of his informal role.

He kept in touch with his former team. Within a few months, the new leader rolled back many of the changes Marcos had instituted. Morale and engagement sank. Less than a year after he'd moved on, management asked Marcos to return to the group.

For the second time in as many years, he left a job he loved for a team whose work he found tedious. To add to his challenges, the group would, once again, have no designated team leader, and Marcos would not get the formal recognition, nor the pay raise, he felt he deserved. It was disappointing, yet deep down, part of him was excited to take on the challenge anyway.

He approached his second time around with big plans. *Even though these people don't report to me, I'm going to rebuild this team and make it work the right way,* he thought. Acting like the leader many of us aspire to be, he set out to tidy the team. It was too big and unproductive, and it had become a place where employees experienced little joy. He set an ambitious goal to reduce an error rate of more than 10 percent to an impressively low 3 percent, while shrinking the group's size. He wanted to make the team so efficient that there would be no way he'd be called into service a third time. "Everybody on the team knows that I'm trying to automate myself out of a job," he boasted.

He helped design a bot to do the equivalent work of five team members, which paved the way to reduce the team's size by more than half. Afterward, he found his teammates better jobs. One moved from the manual and mundane work of fixing invoices to taking over responsibility for the group's meetings. Another finally got the courage to move to a team that could better utilize her skill set. Due to his efforts, the company saved a lot of money and employees were doing work that brought them more joy—a far cry from the monotony of correcting thousands of bills. Marcos felt fulfilled by helping everyone, referring to his work as "absolutely satisfying."

———

When teams are in sync, work feels energizing and our productivity is high. Members are filled with pride and committed to making a difference. But when we find ourselves on a team that's disorganized, we waste time and get frustrated. We may even check out completely, showing up unprepared or unwilling to speak up with our own ideas.

Given the nature of most jobs, it's hard to experience joy at work if the teams you're on aren't joyful. Marcos seized the opportunity to improve his team, even without a formal leadership role. He transformed an inefficient team doing uninspiring work into an organized one doing much more enjoyable and higher-quality work. Although you might not lead a team, you can do your part to make it more joyful!

Visualizing Your Ideal Team

You've probably encountered two types of teams. Primary work teams are permanent groups typically organized around a department area or other organizational need. Examples include a unit of nurses, a battalion of soldiers, or a cross-functional leadership group. Project teams are temporary and are formed to solve a specific problem, launch a product, serve a client, or make a decision. Both types involve collaborating with others, putting together different viewpoints, and generating and implementing ideas.

Take a moment and imagine what your ideal team is like. How does it feel? Is it full of positive interactions and nurturing relationships? Is it a "business only" team that quickly tackles a task, or is there room for connection beyond the work, including hanging out with colleagues? Is your ideal team one that challenges you to do your best work? Does it provide support, encouragement, or growth? There's no right or wrong answer here, as long as it feels right to you.

Make a Teams Pile

It's time to gather up all your teams in a pile. At the top of an index card (or on a spreadsheet), write the name of each team, including your primary work group and all project teams.

Now let's figure out what's going on in each team. Sure, there's the "[blank] task force" or the "generic problem-solving team." But what's the real purpose of these teams? *Purpose* is the genuine belief in the value of the work you are doing. It helps us find meaning in our efforts by connecting us to a larger goal. Without a purpose, teams quickly become messes, straying from task to task, lacking a clear reason to exist.

The team leader is supposed to outline a team's purpose—and if you're that person, get going! The rest of us want to understand a team's purpose, even if we've never been told of it, so we can feel like our efforts add up to something and our time is well spent. Simply saying "to grow," "to solve problems," or "to improve the process" is way too vague. It's also uninspiring. In the most concrete way you can, connect the team's work to helping a person or group. For Marcos's invoice-corrections team, it wasn't about fixing mistakes. His team felt the call to restore integrity to the company by paying vendors accurately and in a timely manner. A product-development team is at its best when its purpose isn't just launching products but delighting customers and making their lives better.

In one truly inspiring study, researchers observed a team of hospital cleaners. Their job was to maintain patient rooms and public spaces, an often messy task and one that usually has unhappy employees. Yet this team was thriving, and employees loved their jobs. Their secret? Instead of narrowly defining their team's purpose as cleaning up after patients, they saw themselves as offering critical care to the sick. Besides providing a comfortable environment for patients undergoing difficult treatments, the team made patients feel better, for example, by handing out tissues to people crying or a glass of water to those suffering from nausea.

Write a sentence on each index card summarizing the purpose for each team you serve on. Ask yourself: *What contributions does our team make to the company's goals or vision? What useful information or ideas are we generating? What do I personally enjoy about participating on the team?*

Are you struggling to answer these questions? Talk with others on the team about how they view the team's purpose. If you're still struggling, there might not be a reason for the team to exist. Some teams may have had a purpose in the past—but they've already met it.

Evaluate Your Teams Pile

Now pick up each index card, moving from the easiest one to consider to the most difficult. For most, that will mean starting with the team you're least involved with and ending with your primary work group. Ask these questions for each team:

Is the team required for my job? Unless you're changing jobs, you'll need to stay engaged with your primary work team. Other teams need to be kept because they provide information needed to get your work done, your input is required, or simply because your boss demands it.

Does the team help move me closer to my ideal work life? Maybe it motivates you or will equip you with the skills or connections for the joyful future you want.

Does it bring joy? For example, is working toward the team's purpose itself joyful?

Before putting a card down, recognize that no matter how bad a team feels at times, there's usually something to value in it. What can you learn from someone on the team? Who are you closest to and enjoy talking with the most? What kind of work do you perform for the team that is worthwhile?

Sort the teams into two piles: those you're happy with and those that need improvement. If your primary work team sparks joy, that's a terrific place to be, as it's usually the one where you spend the most time. If a specific project team is bringing you joy, what's drawing you to it? Knowing the source of joy will help you learn more about yourself and what you'd like to get out of work.

As much as I'd like to share with you a trick to discard the pile of joyless teams, that's not practical for most people. What is possible is to make the team better — and a source of greater joy (and less frustration). Focus on this pile of teams, but the advice I'm offering can also make a good team even better. Remember, no matter your job title, there are some simple ways to make a team more joyful.

Don't Create Messes for Your Teammates

One checked-out team member can quickly turn a joyful team into a messy one where everyone becomes disengaged. Nobody wants to put in extra effort to make up for team members who slack off and show up unprepared. Free-riding is toxic for a team's atmosphere. "Why should I work hard, when so-and-so isn't working hard?" the reasoning typically goes. When this attitude spreads, teams become a mess. Beyond the finger-pointing and defensiveness, fewer people show up prepared and even fewer deliver their best work. Those who work extra to pick up the slack start to feel resentful and may burn out.

There's an explanation for why people check out of teams, and it's usually not because they're lazy or irresponsible. Have you ever not participated in a team because you thought others were smarter, knew more, or had greater experience? A lack of confidence often blinds people to the unique treasures they bring to work. It's often the least-experienced person on a team who can help solve the hardest challenges. Don't let the false belief that you have nothing to contribute sideline you from participating—and create a team atmosphere that looks like you're not fully present. Help build confidence by letting everyone know (including yourself!) that they have a valuable contribution to make. Be specific by identifying one thing they do that truly makes a difference to you, the team, another member of the organization, or a customer.

Trust Keeps Teams Tidy

In today's fast-paced work world, trusting one another helps people avoid burning out and bringing work problems home—returning grumpy, with little time to spend with loved ones who deserve the energy you don't have. Besides creating a much more pleasant work environment, trust helps teams reach important goals. When you're in a group with high trust, everyone tries to better the collective. In low-trust groups, those efforts go toward individual goals, usually at the expense of the group. The result: a messy team full of arguments that spends a lot of time accomplishing very little.

Trust is difficult to build at the moment it's needed, so don't wait. Spend time getting to know team members outside the office. Openly share information that encourages others to reciprocate. Don't be quick to blame other team members for mistakes, as they'll be less willing to admit to them in the future. Instead, candidly talk about previous mishaps and learn from them. And admit to your own mistakes. Once we acknowledge our own limitations, we stop being so hard on ourselves for every small slip. This creates a much safer environment where we can all fess up to our shortcomings for the betterment of the group.

Disagreements Don't Always Make a Mess

It's relaxing to be in a room with a bunch of people who agree with you. The problem: If they don't disagree, they're likely not fully analyzing a decision or generating a rich discussion. What won't be relaxing is when the team underdelivers because people were afraid to raise an opposing viewpoint. This is commonly referred to as groupthink, and teams like this perform poorly. For the best outcome, you'll need to get comfortable talking to people with different views.

Even with diverse teams, research shows that people tend to focus on what everyone knows in common, for example, the client preferences, prior projects, and the typical way the company operates. Despite the fact that we tend to talk about what we know in common, each person also brings distinct knowledge. It's often these seemingly small bits of information that prove vital for an effective team. Everyone on a team can do their part by bringing their unique experiences, ideas, and backgrounds to the work.

If you find that the group is in too much agreement over ideas, assign someone to play the devil's advocate. By explicitly accepting the role, you'll feel safe pushing back on other members' ideas and pointing out missed perspectives. Just make sure you give others the opportunity to try out this role. It will bring in new perspectives, and it's not fun always having to be the skeptic.

If you're still struggling to generate different ideas, don't do one thing that teams frequently turn to: brainstorming. Brainstormed ideas often fall short of their promise because the sessions in which they're produced combine both generation and evaluation of ideas. While trying to create a safe, respectful atmosphere where everyone can keep proposing ideas, it's all too common to dismiss an idea before it has even had the chance to develop. After a few rounds of watching others' ideas quickly sacked, it's no surprise that some people decide to remain silent. It's also hard not to take negative comments made about our ideas as personal criticism.

Instead of brainstorming, make a suggestion to replace brain-storming with brainwriting—the written generation of ideas within the group. It's an initially silent exercise that can produce the same benefits as brainstorming without its costs. The generation of ideas is separated from the evaluation of those ideas. It's pretty simple to do. Ask team members to silently write their ideas on note cards. After an idea-generation period (usually around fifteen minutes), a team member takes responsibility for grouping similar note-card ideas together. Each idea is then anonymously presented to the entire team and evaluated.

Clean Up Personal Conflicts

If a team has too much conflict due to personality differences or political posturing, it can do real harm to both the team as a whole and its individual members. Nobody wants to be the target of or even a spectator to a lot of fighting and personal attacks. Talk about a joyless environment!

Steer clear of getting drawn into other people's drama. Avoid gossiping or speaking negatively about others. And don't be tricked into thinking that complaining about someone with other teammates creates a real and lasting bond. Any intimacy that does arise is false, short-term, and damaging to your integrity.

Recognize that when someone challenges an idea, it doesn't mean they don't like you or are mean-spirited. I know that's hard. Our pride and insecurities can make unflattering comments about our ideas feel like a personal attack—even if there are no bad intentions. If the team worked to build trust beforehand, it's got some protection. Trust turns disagreements over ideas into productive conversations, while making us feel better about hearing the news.

Clean up any messes you're responsible for by resolving personal conflicts. It sometimes requires you to take the high road in order to clear the air. I know how hard it can be to approach someone to say, "I'd like for us to be great partners and to support each other's work. I can see I haven't been fully acting that way, and I'm sorry." More often than not, the other person will reciprocate your gesture of good will. If they don't, they might have what researchers call an egocentric orientation—a strong individualistic focus—that blinds them to your goodwill gesture. Give it one more shot, this time more explicitly laying out your desire to overcome past differences.

Big Teams Are Usually Full of Clutter

Big teams can create big messes. Research shows that larger teams are less satisfying than smaller ones. With so many other people around, there's a good chance that there will be a lot of overlap in members' contributions, making it more likely that teams become chaotic and disorganized. Also, it's hard to stand out and see the impact of our own work with too many people around.

A bigger team is also almost always a slower one. Trying to

reach a consensus with a big team takes a lot of time, and sometimes it isn't even possible. Amazon.com CEO Jeff Bezos lives by the "two-pizza rule"—no team should be large enough that it needs to be fed with more than two pizzas. Research backs up Bezos's rule of thumb. Studies peg the optimal size for most teams from four to six people if they're trying to generate ideas, make decisions, or innovate, with teams of more than nine people pushing the limits of what's effective.

Although it's usually up to the team leader to determine its size, knowing the drawbacks of larger teams can help anyone. When on a larger team, propose breaking out into smaller working groups. Don't be so quick to recommend another team member who doesn't offer a unique perspective. And when you're in charge, aim to create small teams.

KonMari's Secret to Joyful Team Building

Sparking joy at work is important to the KonMari team. The first step we take is to identify what kinds of things spark joy for each team member and then delegate jobs accordingly. Our executive assistant, Kay, for example, loves managing tasks on Excel and tackling them systematically. She's also very good at handling little details that

---

need to be dealt with right away, so these are the kinds of things we always ask her to do. She's the type of person who gets energized the more she works.

Jocelyn, our social media community manager, has a keen interest in making a social impact, so rather than focusing on increases in the number of followers, I always share with her the ways in which our work makes the world a better place.

Andrea loves to make customers happy, so she is the one we ask to handle communications with our clients. At our weekly company meeting, she has an opportunity to share what she has done that week to make our customers happy, called the Wow Moment. This always boosts the team's motivation.

As for Takumi, my husband, what makes him happy is interacting with others and creating a work environment that allows everyone to tap into their strengths. He is currently in charge of team management while also serving as my producer. This job is such a perfect fit, I think it must be his calling in life.

If we want to enjoy our work and be highly productive, it's important to know what our passion is, to share that with the rest of the team, and to know what sparks joy for them, too. **M.K.**

———

Although teams can be a source of joy for all their members, they too commonly fall short of their promise. Know that the success of a team is everyone's responsibility, no matter their job title, seniority, or tenure—and a privilege for us to enjoy at work. Do your best to tidy your teams, and you'll bring joy not just to yourself but to everyone else in the group.

CHAPTER 10

Sharing the Magic of Tidying

You might wonder why you should maintain a neat desk if there's a messy common space around the corner. Or you might question why you tidied your calendar if the corporate culture regularly permits others to fill it up again. And keeping up with your inbox in a company packed with email junkies can challenge even the most determined digital tidier. Here's the thing: By organizing your work, you've given yourself a gift that goes far beyond a tidy desk, orderly calendar, or clean inbox. You've taken back some control of your work life. So what's next?

Share the magic of tidying with others!

It's easy to think we can't change much when we're not in charge. People are quick to criticize a company's top leaders for contributing to all the messes we face at work—and in some cases, the boss deserves a fair share of the blame. But instead of watching from the sidelines, focus on what you can do to make things better.

Small actions can bring surprisingly big changes to an organization. Never think that you're not important enough or senior enough to make a difference. You are! Just be realistic. Company cultures don't change overnight. Instead, spread the joy that comes from tidying, one step at a time.

Let Your Tidying Inspire Others

My office used to be a mess…a big mess. I had way too many books, even for a professor. I hadn't touched most of them for years. Stacks of research articles piled so high, they blocked my view. My desk drawers rivaled a bad convenience store — snacks well past their prime and years-old office supplies still in their packaging. I even had a mysterious key: to this day, I have no idea what it opened.

I had very little motivation to tidy until I finished writing my first book, *Stretch*. I found that many people I would talk with asked how my work related to the KonMari Method. Honestly, I was initially surprised by these questions. I had the evidence that showed how making the most out of what you already have fosters creativity, high work performance, and ultimately a better life. I knew Marie was a highly esteemed author and tidying expert, but how could a method that teaches people to clean up their homes relate to making people more successful and satisfied at work?

When *Well + Good* magazine put out its top-ten list of the most exciting books to read in 2017, they added *Stretch* to the list and called it "next-level Marie-Kondo-ing." Curious but still a little skeptical, I decided to experiment with my office and try tidying. I experienced firsthand the powerful transformation from using the method, realizing that it's much more about the process of self-discovery than the actual acts of organizing. A neat space stands out and gets people interested in tidying. But it's learning about yourself that brings you closer to the life you want.

After I tidied my office, my colleagues were absolutely shocked. "Wow, what happened?" they asked. "Your office looks amazing!" They, too, wanted a space filled with items they loved. Sharing my office was just the beginning. I had higher ambitions for people to tidy all aspects of their work.

This is where you can help. Although you can't force tidying upon others, you can inspire them by sharing all that you've accomplished. Invite colleagues to check out your workspace. Talk about your approach to managing your email and calendar. Show off your smartphone and computer desktop. Let people know how you've avoided getting bogged down by too many decisions. Keep building high-quality connections, and people will be moved to make their own. Explain how and why you politely request a meeting agenda.

If you can, go one step further. Propose a tidying day to the company's leaders so that everyone in the office can transform their workspaces. For meetings, suggest for one day per week canceling all but the most essential meetings and try to shorten the ones you still need to have. Use the saved time to work on anything that sparks joy. Recommend that everyone in the company lay off email for one coordinated hour each day; that will provide needed relief from constant interruptions. Then build a supportive community of work tidiers to learn about new tidying techniques and motivate one another to keep going.

Show Care for the Workplace

If you're like most people, you've probably passed a stray piece of paper on the floor and moved on. When did you last see a dirty dish in the office break room and leave it there? Have you ever come to a meeting room only to find the whiteboard wasn't wiped clean? These messes are not big deals themselves. But they signal a lack of care.

Over time, small messes can turn into larger ones. In one study, researchers compared a tidy shared workroom with a messy one. After a brief period of time, the messy one had three times as much additional clutter as the tidy one. Once the clutter barrier is broken, it's all too easy for people to keep piling it on. That's true for any category you tidy at work, for example, inviting too many people to a meeting or sending an excessive number of emails. Soon enough, everyone's adding to the clutter.

My father was a businessman who owned a motel. When I was a kid, I used to go to work with him a few days during the summer. As we walked around, he would always pick up trash in the hallways. One day I asked him why he bothered when he was the boss and had plenty of housekeepers. He calmly told me, "Caring for the space is everyone's job, from the housekeepers up to the boss." The lesson that everyone counts has stuck with me ever since.

Don't put undue pressure on yourself to be the company's caretaker. You're not. Instead, ask yourself: *What small things can I do to show care for the workplace?* It could be as simple as occasionally cleaning up a dish in the kitchen. If a meeting is turning into a mess—think lots of tangents and political posturing—what can you say to get it back on track? If an email chain has gotten out of control, how can you focus it?

Treasure Your Coworkers

Through tidying, you've learned the importance of taking care of the things in your life. That's even truer of the people you work with. Too often, we take our colleagues for granted (and they take us for granted). The work they deliver, the effort they make, and their contribution to the company environment are unquestionably important for our own success and satisfaction.

It's all too easy to forget that the person you're trying to politically outmaneuver or with whom you're arguing or fighting over resources is a person worthy of respect. Treat him or her that way — and chances are he or she will treat you that way, too. You'll both be better off.

Are you treasuring your coworkers? Using a scale of (1) Never, (2) Rarely, (3) Sometimes, (4) Very Often, or (5) Always, how much do you:

____ express thanks to others?

____ recognize others' important contributions?

____ honor, make space for, and encourage people to be themselves?

____ give people the benefit of the doubt?

____ treat others as worthy of your respect?

Add up your score, and if it totals less than 20, you've got room to do better: Acknowledge others' presence, listen, speak candidly, and just treat everyone you encounter as a person worthy of your respect and recognition. When it comes to how we interact with others, power, status, money, fame, and fortune shouldn't make a difference in how we treat people. Help create an environment that respects everybody by exemplifying a key lesson from tidying: be grateful.

Don't mistake gratitude for perks provided by your organization. When I worked at a startup in Silicon Valley, my company regularly provided free breakfast and dinner. At first, I thought this was a great way of thanking employees for their hard work—and I eagerly looked forward to what was on the menu each night. Over time, it became clear that this was a way of extending our workday. I would often drag my work out, knowing there was dinner waiting for me, which interfered with my evenings and even my sleep.

I often hear from people that they don't feel appreciated. It's not the free dinner or company swag they're after—it's recognition for their work. A congratulations for a job well done. An acknowledgment for taking time away from family to put in the extra effort. Do your part by genuinely thanking people for their contributions, whether you're the boss or the most junior person in the group.

A recent survey of two thousand Americans finds that most people believe that expressing gratitude to a coworker makes them feel happier and more fulfilled. Yet that same survey finds that on a given day, only 10 percent of employees express gratitude to someone at work. The result: so many actions—big and small—go unnoticed and unrecognized, despite the joy that comes from giving and receiving gratitude. Research also finds that receiving gratitude makes employees more engaged at work and more likely to help out their colleagues.

Expressing authentic gratitude takes almost no time and costs little. At one fifteen-hundred-person company that sells made-to-order T-shirts and other merchandise, they use

"WOWs" for expressing gratitude for things employees do. Anyone can send a WOW to a colleague, for seemingly small accomplishments (an expression of thanks for doing something extra to help a customer) to major milestones (completing an important project). What's most important is that the WOWs are detailed. Specificity conveys sincerity and shows that you're really paying attention.

If your organization doesn't have a formal way to facilitate expressing gratitude, do it yourself. There are so many wonderful contributions that people make at work, and they're easy to overlook amid the daily grind. Pause and look around. What do you see?

When was the last time you genuinely thanked a colleague for something they did? After a meeting, say thank you to those who attended and be specific about why their input was helpful. Give credit publicly to people who contributed to projects. Compliment someone.

———

Tell your colleagues about your tidying journey and fill the rest of the office with more joy. Teach your techniques to those who want to learn. Share how tidying has transformed your work and life—and you'll soon have others eager to transform their own.

As we close the book, Marie will provide you with some final tips to spark even more joy at work. She'll also reveal small changes she's made that have had a big impact on her work life.

CHAPTER 11

How to Spark Even More Joy at Work

We have covered a broad range of themes in this book, including how to tidy your office, digital data, time, decisions, networks, meetings, and teams. In this final chapter, I share points I keep in mind and certain things I do to make my work spark even more joy, as well as things I have learned from others that I would like to incorporate into my work.

Caring for What We Keep Improves Work Performance

When I was still working at the staffing agency, the first thing I did when I reached the office was to clean my workspace. I put down my bag, took a favorite dust cloth from a drawer, and wiped the top of my desk. Then I took out my laptop, keyboard, and mouse and gave them a wipe, all while focusing my thoughts on this little phrase: *May today be another great day at work!* I wiped the phone, too, thanking it for always bringing me wonderful opportunities.

Mondays were deep-cleansing days. I got down on my hands and knees, dusted the legs of my chair, then crawled under the desk and wiped the cords. Written out like this, it sounds like a lot of work, but altogether it took less than a minute. Yet it made my desk area look so neat and tidy, it seemed like a world apart. The atmosphere lightened, and it was easier to get down to work. While my hands were busy cleaning, I could empty my mind and make this part of my day into a little meditation, a ritual that allowed me to switch into working mode.

As I continued with these daily practices, my work performance improved, resulting in more deals made and higher sales. That may sound too good to be true, but the number of times I was recognized for improved performance at quarterly meetings definitely increased. Nor was it just me. I have seen countless examples of how caring for the things we use makes work go better. Many clients have reported that after adopting this practice of cleaning their workspace at the start of the day, they noticed that their project proposals were accepted more readily and their sales performance improved.

For some time I pondered the question of why this is so and eventually came to the following conclusions. For starters, if we're going to wipe our desk in the morning, it needs to be neat and tidy already. A tidy desk means that we no longer need to search for a document or think about where to put it when we're done. This improves our work efficiency. In addition, working in an orderly environment feels good, giving us a more positive outlook and allowing ideas and inspirations to flow. But most importantly, I think that when we look after the things that make our work possible, we give off different vibes. Our attitude and behavior toward our clients and coworkers changes, and this naturally leads to better results in our work.

When we care for the things we choose to keep, they give back positive energy. Many years of experience have convinced me that any place where things are treated with respect and gratitude, whether a home or an office, becomes a relaxing and energizing power spot.

To transform a workspace into a power spot that generates constant positive energy, we must first keep it clean. Personally, I like to use a favorite dust cloth or scented cleaning wipes because they help make cleaning an enjoyable habit. While cleaning, remember to express gratitude for the things you use all the time, thanking each item for helping you do your work as you put it back where it belongs.

The ideal is to maintain a state of gratitude throughout the day, starting first thing in the morning by being grateful for everything that makes your work go smoothly. If this doesn't come naturally, however, it's fine to practice thankfulness whenever you remember. One of my clients had a great idea.

She wrote "Thank you always!" on a strip of pretty tape and stuck it to the edge of her computer display to remind herself to be grateful for the tools that helped her do her job.

Believe me, the effect of cherishing your things like this is limitless. Why not transform your workspace into a power spot, too?

Adding More Joy to Your Workspace

"Don't think of it as tidying. Tell yourself it's interior designing." That's what my friend's mother once told her when she was balking at the idea of tidying up. What a great way to describe it. When we tell ourselves that we *have to* do something, it feels like a chore. But when we see tidying as a creative endeavor that will spark joy in our workspace, we're happy to do it.

So when you tackle your workspace, don't think of it as "tidying." Tell yourself that you're designing a joyful place to work. After all, it really is like decorating, especially when you've finished tidying and are choosing your favorite accents. As you tidy, keep your ideal work life in mind and look at what you can do to make this space set your heart dancing.

Take pens, for example. It's only when my clients start tidying that many of them realize they have been using nothing but giveaways. This is your chance to start choosing pens that spark joy for you. And not just pens. When choosing any items you need for daily work, such as your penholder, scissors, or tape, make sure they are ones that you love. Although it may seem ideal to replace everything right away with more attractive items, the best approach is to take your time. Rather than rushing out and buying a bunch of new things that are merely satisfactory, I encourage you to keep looking until you find things that truly spark joy when you just look at or touch them.

In addition, be sure to choose a few things that simply add a touch of joy even though you don't need them for your work. I call this practice "joy plus." You can add anything that lifts your spirits, such as a photo, postcard, or plant you particularly like. As for me, I place a crystal on my desk. Not only does it sparkle, adding beauty, but I find that it also cleanses the atmosphere, making inspiration spring more easily into my mind.

Perhaps the most unusual example of "joy plus" I have encountered in my consulting career was a toothbrush set. This belonged to a company president who kept it displayed on his desk. I have seen many things as a tidying consultant, but this one seemed so strange, I had to ask why. "Even though I'm sitting at my desk, no one will come over to talk if they see me brushing my teeth," he explained. "It's very convenient when I want to concentrate because no one will interrupt me." Just seeing it on his desk brought him joy and a sense of security.

Of course, this example is not the norm. It was a very small company with only two employees and the washroom was located right behind the president's desk. The point is to decorate your desk with whatever sparks joy for you, no matter what that may be.

Speaking of decorating desks, since I began working in the

United States, I have noticed that Americans tend to add more joy-plus touches in the workplace than people in Japan. Japanese workers hesitate to display any personal items at work, whereas it's quite common for Americans to put things like wedding photos or a plant on their desk. I've even seen model airplanes and big helium balloons in people's offices. Although this surprised me at first, it made me realize the importance of adding some playfulness, too.

Of all the offices I've seen in America, Airbnb in San Francisco comes out tops in playfulness. The office encourages employee creativity and values open consultation. There are many small rooms available for employees to work on their own or to use for small meetings. The interior design of each room is inspired by a different place in the world, such as Paris, Sydney, or London. I was quite impressed by the authenticity and attention to detail of the Japan-themed room. It reproduced perfectly the atmosphere of an *izakaya* or pub from the 1950s, complete with red paper lanterns, a *noren* curtain over the entrance, and vintage knickknacks. Of course, the whole building was designed to spark joy, not just the individual rooms, but even if your company's building isn't like that, there are still things you can do to spark joy in your own work area. Below are just a few examples.

- Decide a theme color for coordinating items on your desk.

- Choose a favorite movie or story as a theme for decorating your workspace.
- Find photos online to decorate your desk area.
- Place a small potted plant on your desk.
- Display a photo that brings back joyful memories.
- Add something sparkly, such as a crystal or glass paperweight.
- Keep a small aroma item on your desk that will give just your space a special fragrance.
- Place a beautiful candle on your desk as a decoration.
- Choose a favorite coaster for your drink.
- Change the background on your desktop computer to reflect each season.

How about you? What ideas come to mind for sparking joy in your workspace? Give your imagination free rein and add lots of joy-plus touches.

Should You Change Your Job If It Doesn't Spark Joy?

Tidying quite naturally hones our ability to discern what sparks joy and what doesn't, and we learn to apply this sensitivity to all kinds of things. I know many people who switched jobs or quit to start their own business once they finished tidying their workspace.

When they hear this, people often say, "My current job doesn't spark joy. Should I quit right now and find another?"

One such client was Yu, who worked for a food manufacturer. After tidying up her home and her workspace, she found that what actually sparked joy for her was making accessories.

"The pay at this company is good," she told me, "but I come home exhausted all the time. It's just no fun. I wonder if it would be better to become an accessory designer and start my own business. Or maybe I should switch to a company that makes accessories and crafts."

When clients consult me about this kind of thing, my first response is to encourage them to choose the path that sparks joy for them. Yu, however, had mixed feelings about that. "Accessory designers can't make a living," she said. "And I haven't seen any company that really appeals to me."

My next suggestion was that she do a joy analysis. I encouraged her to examine the different aspects of her job and decide which ones brought her joy and which ones didn't. I also asked her to identify whether or not those aspects were things over which she had control.

When we met again several months later, I was struck by how different she looked. She seemed much more cheerful and relaxed. She told me that after evaluating her job, she had decided to stay put. "When I examined what didn't bring me joy," she explained, "I found that a big part of it was having to commute during peak rush hours. It was exhausting. Instead, I started coming in an hour earlier. That drastically reduced my fatigue in the morning, and I was able to work far more efficiently.

"Another factor was a client that I really didn't like. Gathering up my courage, I consulted my boss, and someone else was put in charge. By changing those things that could be changed, I was able to eliminate many of those that sucked the pleasure out of my work. Now I really enjoy my job. Of course, not everything sparks joy, but I realized that the best work-life balance for me is to make a decent salary while pursuing my passion for accessory design in my spare time."

If, like Yu, you're wondering if you should change jobs, I encourage you to analyze your current situation first. When we encounter difficulties at work, whether in our relationships with coworkers or clients or in our job responsibilities, those problems often originate from a combination of factors. We need to examine and deal with each one. What sparks joy for you at work right now, and what doesn't? What can be changed, and what can't? Take an objective look at your situation and your approach and consider what you need to do to achieve a joyful work style. There may still be things you can do to improve your situation.

Whether you decide to stay in your current job, find a new one, or quit and launch your own business, assessing and coming to terms with your present reality is excellent preparation for your next step. That's something I've learned through my experience in tidying. Taking a new step always entails letting something go and saying goodbye. That's why it's so important to prepare your mind first. Maybe it's because of the stress involved, but ironically, when we treat things that don't spark joy with disdain, when we chuck them while focusing on how we don't want or need them and call them useless junk, we are likely to end up buying more of the same kind of thing and facing similar problems.

So when you decide not to keep something, focus on the good it brought you and let it go with gratitude for the connection you had with it. The positive energy you direct at that item will attract new and joyful encounters. The same principle applies when considering a job change. Think of your job positively, with gratitude, recognizing that although it may have been hard, it taught you such things as the importance of keeping a certain distance in your relationships, or that it was thanks to this experience that you could find the work style that's best for you. This kind of attitude will lead you to the job that is just right for the next stage in your life.

Enjoy the Process of Creating a Joyful Work Life

Of all the people I have met, the one who seems to enjoy his work the most is the well-known Japanese calligrapher and artist Souun Takeda, who also wrote the calligraphy used in this book's cover design. Until I met him, my image of a calligrapher was of someone very serious wielding a brush with great solemnity and a deeply furrowed brow. Souun, however, is the exact opposite. He loves his work wholeheartedly.

"I never suffer any birth pangs when producing new works," he says. "It's kind of like burping. I don't know why, but they just seem to pop out." What a unique and lighthearted approach. At forty-two, he's a prolific and sought-after artist, but his success didn't come automatically. He started at the age of three, learning from his mother, a professional calligrapher herself. His first job after university was in the sales department of a major IT company. When he quit and started his career as an independent calligrapher, he had a hard time getting clients. So although his work now sparks the ultimate joy, reaching this place took time and effort.

That's true for me, too. Tidying comes as naturally as breathing. And it's so much fun. Yet it hasn't all been smooth sailing. My passion for tidying began at the age of five, but it took me many years of trial and error to develop my method and reach where I am today. Now I share my method with people around the world through talks, books, TV, and other media. This part of my work is not always fun, and I still encounter many challenges. When I think about it, though, it's been less than ten years since I started sharing my method more widely with others, so it makes sense that I'm not as good at this as I am at tidying. But I have been learning and evolving as I go along.

After I quit the staffing agency and went independent, for example, only four people signed up for my first seminar, and two out of those four canceled at the last minute. In the large, almost empty seminar room, I struggled to get my points across, painfully aware of my own inexperience. I felt so miserable and so sorry for the poor participants that I longed to run away and hide.

This experience taught me that I lacked marketing skills. I

began reading as many books as I could find on PR and business management, went to seminars, made connections by joining morning gatherings for businesspeople, and started a regular blog to get exposure. Instead of trying to attract large numbers, I started out smaller, holding seminars in community centers for groups of up to ten people in tatami-mat rooms where we sat on the floor Japanese-style.

Later, I opened my own booth at wellness events. To make sure I stood out, I wore a cotton kimono known as a *yukata* and stuck a broad fan in my sash emblazoned with the words "Let me solve your tidying problems!" I would wander around the site dressed like this to advertise my services.

Through pursuing such strategies, I gradually reached the point where I could hold monthly seminars for thirty that were filled to capacity. The number of my individual clients also began increasing. When my waiting list grew to be six months long, people began asking me to write a book about my tidying method, and that led to publishing my first book.

Of course, after I published it, and even today when I speak to audiences that number several thousand, I still encounter new challenges. But with each passing year, I can see that the more experience I gain, the greater the ratio of joy I find in my work.

Work is based on accumulated experience. Through working, we grow. Nothing is all thrills right from the start. Even if something is not going well or doesn't feel right at this moment, if it is leading you toward a future that sparks joy, then think of it as a growing pain. If your work life doesn't spark joy all the time, don't assume that you're a failure. Instead, recognize the potential of this moment to bring you closer to your ideal, enjoy the process, and celebrate the fact that you're still growing. Be confident that you are creating a joyful work life right now through the daily process of acquiring experience.

When the Fear of Others' Opinions Holds You Back

Tidying up can help you get a clear picture of the path that sparks joy for you. You come to see what's close to your heart, what you've always wanted to do, and what challenges you want to take on. But when it comes to actually setting foot on that path, you may feel some trepidation along with your excitement. Many people discover something they want to try but are held back because they worry about what others might think.

I know this from my own experience. My life mission is to increase the number of people who live a life that sparks joy through tidying up. For that reason, I write books, give talks, and appear in the media. A few years ago when I reviewed my mission, I felt it was time to start sharing my ideas on social media to reach more people. But just the thought of doing that was terrifying. I worried that if I presented my thoughts and lifestyle on such an open forum, I might become the target of negative criticism or hatred. For a long time, I couldn't even bring myself to set up a social media account.

Finally, I consulted Jinnosuke Kokoroya, a well-known therapist in Japan. He also happens to be an old friend, and our families enjoy spending time together. "I'd really like to start using social media to get my message out there," I told him, "but I can't bring myself to do it. I'm afraid that people might hate me and start attacking me."

Jinnosuke smiled and said, "Don't worry, Marie. Plenty of people hate you already." This, by the way, is what he tells all his clients who are afraid of being hated. That's his approach.

I bet he's right, I thought. Timidly, I searched for my name online. After my official website and blog, the highest-ranking article was "Why We Hate Marie Kondo." I was stunned, but thanks to this, my thinking changed 180 degrees. The fear of others' opinions had held me back from using social media, but now I realized that there was no point in caring. Whether I used social media or not, people were criticizing me already.

I stopped and asked myself, *Does it really spark joy to reject the path that calls me because I'm afraid of being criticized?* The answer was a resounding *No!* My inner voice cried out, *I want to share joy through the KonMari Method with as many people as possible.* I immediately set up instagram@marie kondo and other social media accounts. In the end, there wasn't as much criticism as I had expected, and the number of people who supported my decision to venture into social media kept growing. Information and positive news items that I posted began making it into the top online search rankings. Although I was worried at the time, I'm now really glad that I had the courage to take that first step.

There are many different types of people, perspectives, and value systems in this world, so we can't expect to be liked or understood by everyone. It's only natural that some people will criticize. No matter what we do or how decently we might behave, someone is bound to misunderstand. What a waste, then, to choose a lifestyle that doesn't spark joy just for fear of being criticized.

You get only one chance at life. Which will you choose? To live in fear of what others might think? Or to follow your own heart?

Let Go of the Past to Enjoy the Future

Too often we clutter our mind with our biggest fears, anxieties, past failures, and criticism from others. Although most of us experience more positive events than negative ones, we remember the bad ones — and they have an outsize impact on our mental health. When we're self-critical, we become less confident. Fixating on real or imagined failure puts us on a course to fail in the future because we're so distracted thinking about our "flaws." It also makes it harder to pursue our work-life vision, or any goal for that matter, because we're preoccupied with past mistakes and concerned about making future ones. Stop wasting mental energy ruminating about the past, comparing what you have or do to others, or dwelling on a mistake that happened last week. To discard a negative thought, write it down on a piece of paper. Honor its message by thinking about it. Take a key lesson from it. Ask how it can contribute to your growth by being a learning opportunity. Then dispose of the paper (shred it, burn it, bury it), and the thought will disappear along with it. You've learned from the bad thought—keep the lesson but discard the self-criticism.   **S.S.**

Make Time for Honest Self-Reflection

Of all the people I have met, my husband, Takumi Kawahara, is the person who comes to mind first when I think of someone whose work is tidy. He also happens to be the cofounder and CEO of KonMari Media, Inc., as well as my producer.

When I say his "work is tidy," I mean that he is always clear about what needs to be done, carries out his tasks efficiently, and works stress-free with joy. In contrast, when people's work is not tidy, it means that they are swamped with tasks that have to be done and experience a lot of stress while working.

Takumi sets aside a slot of time for office work and focuses on it until it's all done. He also deals with every task that comes his way immediately so that the ball is back in the other person's court. Twice a week he goes to the gym to stay fit. He keeps up-to-date with the latest books and movies, plays with our daughters, does the housework, and still makes time to just relax. I'm the complete opposite. When I'm writing a book, I often find myself feeling exhausted and overwhelmed by deadlines.

So how does he manage to get his work done properly and on time yet still have plenty of time to lie around at home like a big, cuddly teddy bear, looking at his cell phone? His working style is such an enviable example of "joy at work" that I decided to ask him his secret. His reply was simply this: "I make sure to take time for honest self-reflection."

Every two weeks he sets aside an hour or so to reflect on why he is working, what he hopes to achieve through his work, and what his ideal work life is. Based on that, he prioritizes all the tasks he is currently doing and then spends ten minutes every morning deciding which ones he will tackle that day before starting work. (I'm sure I'm not the only one amazed at the frequency and amount of time he devotes to this!)

This kind of planning is only part of it. He also says it's crucial to reflect on his actions so that he can revise and improve. He applies the 80/20 rule daily—the idea that 80 percent of results in business and life come from just 20 percent of our efforts. He assesses his tasks and eliminates those that are unnecessary and unproductive, focusing instead on those that are productive. For example, if he feels that we are having too many meetings about the ideal work life, he'll reduce the number from four to two a month or shorten the meetings from sixty minutes to fifty, so that he can devote extra time and energy to the most productive work.

Not only does he prioritize work tasks, but he also prioritizes whom he spends time with. His first priority is to make sure that he gets time with himself for self-reflection. This is followed by time with his family, including me and our children, our employees, business partners, and clients. He says that good relationships with the people closest to him result in a better attitude, clearer communication (which reduces problems caused by miscommunication), and increased productivity. In the end, all these things lead to providing better services to our customers.

I was surprised to learn that he developed this approach while he was still an employee at another company, not after becoming an executive officer in our company. I'm sure he has been able to spark joy at work because he has made it a habit to take time for self-reflection, assess his current situation, and make improvements.

Ways We Tidy Up Work as a Couple

Influenced by Takumi and the kind of person he is, I now make time to reflect with him whenever I find tasks piling up and my workload increasing, or whenever I feel that my productivity is dropping. As a couple, we tidy up our work using the following three steps.

Step 1: Grasp reality.

We take a big sketchbook, turn it sideways, and draw a horizontal line across the top of the page. We split that line into twelve equal sections with the names of the months and write in anything that has been decided for our schedule during that year. For example, "March: Talk in New York," "May: Filming for TV show," "August: Book publication." In the space beneath, we jot down ideas for projects that we would like to do but for which the timing has not yet been decided. This gives us a clear overall picture of current and upcoming projects at that point in time.

Step 2: Prioritize projects and decide the time frame.

The next step is to decide the order of importance for each project. To do this, we ask ourselves questions such as: *Does it spark joy? Will it lead to joy in the future? Is this something that has to be done regardless of whether or not it sparks joy?* When deciding if it will lead to a joyful future, we consider whether it will help us reach our goal and realize our corporate philosophy, which in our case is to "organize the world."

Once our projects are prioritized, we consider how much time to devote to each and write that into our sketchbook schedule. Our basic policy is to allot most of our energy to work that sparks joy and that leads to a joyful future and to spend only the minimum required on work that has to be done regardless.

When every project has been written into the sketchbook, we look it over. If we notice that there's too much time devoted to publishing-related work or that we need to take some action to increase brand awareness, we adjust the amount of time allotted for each project and task accordingly.

Step 3: Break projects down into tasks.

The above two steps give us an overall picture, including the order of priority for every project and about how much time each one will require. Our third step is to break each project down into more detailed tasks and write these into our Google calendar or datebook. When we're done, we do a final sweep of our schedule. If we decide that a task recorded there has low priority, we adjust our schedule by eliminating that task or moving it to another time period. In this way, we create a schedule that includes only those tasks that are the most meaningful and rewarding.

Our basic approach to tidying up work can be applied to a three-year period instead of just one year, or it can be used to examine a single project in greater detail. Once I began tidying my work in this way, I started to realize how meaningful everyday tasks are. This helped to boost my motivation and also increased my level of concentration. Through this process of tidying up work with Takumi, I learned that my joy level and motivation rise dramatically when I approach each task, no matter how small, with an appreciation of its significance.

Your Work and Your Life Are the Sum of Your Choices

Soon after I began working on the world stage, I became so busy that I barely had time to think. My husband is also my manager, and I felt like I was complaining to him all the time. On a good day, I would grumble, "My schedule's so tight, there's no time to rest! And without any rest, how can I possibly do a good job?" But on a bad day, when my stress level was at the max, I said things that I'm ashamed to even write down. "My staff and my clients, everyone seems happy but me!" I would say. "Here I am telling people how important joy is, but there's no joy for me."

Whenever I got like this, Takumi would say, "Marie, if you really don't want to do this, you can quit anytime. If you want to cancel that talk, I'll contact the organizer and apologize. If you don't like working in an organization, we can fold up the company." His tone was calm and totally neutral, without the slightest trace of sarcasm or disappointment, and he never tried to pressure me.

His words always brought me back to my senses. That talk, I would remember, was something I had accepted eagerly as a good opportunity. Starting a company in America was my own choice; that's what I really wanted to do. All of these things were steps along the path I chose because I long to spread the KonMari Method and share the joy it can spark in our lives.

During tidying lessons, when my clients just can't bring themselves to discard a certain item, I always advise them to keep it with confidence. If it's a purse that doesn't spark joy but was so expensive they can't let it go, I encourage them not to hide it in the back of the closet, but to line it up right alongside those bags that do spark joy. Rather than bombarding it with negative thoughts every time they see it, I suggest they send it a loving glance and thank it for being there.

When we resolve to keep something with this attitude, that choice will naturally lead to one of two outcomes: we'll find that the item we kept has played its role to its conclusion and we're ready to let it go, or our fondness for it will grow, raising it to the rank of something that truly sparks joy. This applies not just to physical tidying, but to every choice we make. Keeping things consciously, telling ourselves that we deliberately chose to keep them because that's what we wanted to do, enables us to either let things go with gratitude or keep and treasure them.

Our work and our lives are the cumulative result of our past choices. Whatever happens is the result of our own decisions. If something you're engaged in doesn't bring you joy, remember that where you are now is the path that you chose in the past. Based on that understanding, ask yourself what you want to do next. If you choose to let something go, do it with gratitude. If you choose to continue, do it with conviction. Whatever your decision, if it is made deliberately and with confidence, it will surely contribute to a joyful life.

You Deserve a Joyful Job

Knowing what sparks joy at work provides a guide for moving your job closer to your work-life vision. Enjoy your tidier workspace. Use the extra time and mental energy tidying created to do tasks that bring greater joy. Do more joy projects by volunteering outside your core responsibilities for activities that spark joy. Emphasize and master those activities that do bring joy (even if you need to keep other activities that don't bring joy). Try spending more time with colleagues who bring joy, and do your best to avoid those who don't.

If these efforts still fail to spark joy, you might need a more substantial change. If your job brings joy but your organization doesn't, consider a new place to work. If your colleagues bring you joy but your position does not, consider a better-fitting job within the same organization. If you believe you've tapped out the full potential of your current occupational choice, consider a new type of work. Be careful, however. The grass often looks greener on the other side, and there's usually a lot of untapped potential and unrealized joy where you're already working.

Whether you stay or leave, don't hold on to the past ("This is the way I've always worked") or be fearful of the future ("If I don't do this work, what will I do?"). The way you do your current job might feel comfortable, but if it's no longer joyful, take action. With much more awareness of your work-life vision and how to achieve it, you're going to approach your next career choice with the right priorities.   **S.S.**

Maintaining Work-Life Balance

Our lives as a couple changed completely when we had children. Before our first daughter was born, I envisioned my ideal lifestyle like this: I would awake refreshed in the morning, get dressed, and have breakfast ready before the children woke up. I would complete my work for the day so quickly and efficiently that there would be plenty of time left to play with the children. In the evening, I would make dinner, pouring into it all my love and affection, and we would then sit down to enjoy it together as a family. At bedtime, I would do some yoga and relax before falling asleep, feeling pleasantly tired. And of course, my house would always be tidy!

That was my ideal, but life is not that easy. Once I gave birth, I had no time and no emotional space. My expectations and aspirations dropped to the level of being satisfied if I was able to brush my teeth before I went to bed and being relieved just to know that my children were alive. Babies wake up often and early, so I never got enough sleep. I was always tired, my ability to concentrate dropped markedly, and I couldn't get my work or the chores done on time. I tried to keep our home neat and tidy, but the kids would dump a bag of salt all over the floor or open up the drawers and mess up my writing tools, which were neatly organized into compartments. No matter how much I tidied, the house quickly reverted to clutter.

Once, after I taught my daughters how to fold clothes, they pulled out everything that I had put neatly away in the drawers, "folded" them all over again, and put them back. It looked perfect to them but of course not to me! I'm sure they just wanted to try folding by themselves, but I couldn't see any humor in it at the time. I scolded them harshly, only to mentally kick myself later for my impatience. This situation didn't spark even a "j," let alone "joy." Things calmed down only once they started school.

Raising toddlers can be really hard, but it taught me a valuable lesson: Don't aim to keep things perfectly tidy when your children are little. At the same time, however, I did make a point of at least keeping some of my own personal space tidy, such as making sure that the drawers of the desk in my office were neat or that the way I hung the clothes in my closet sparked joy. With children, we have a lot less control over many aspects of daily life. For this very reason, it's important to make the spaces over which we do have control spark joy. Creating a place, even just one, that sparks joy for us each time we're in it can really change how we feel.

It's common everywhere for people raising young children to feel overwhelmed, and I often receive letters from working parents asking me for advice. One of the most common questions is "How can I create a good work-life balance?" I always respond with this suggestion: "Start by visualizing your ideal work-life balance."

As I mentioned earlier, once Takumi and I had children, our work-life balance changed dramatically. It became physically impossible for us to work long hours, because we needed to spend more time and energy on our children. And because we could no longer stick to our previous lifestyle, we began discussing together what kind of work-life balance would make us happy.

In our case, we chose to prioritize time for ourselves and for our family, then scheduled our work around that. Naturally, this meant we had to turn down more projects than before, but we let these opportunities go with gratitude, thanking those who had approached us and expressing our hope that we could work with them in the future if the timing was right. This allowed us to recharge our batteries, which in turn helped us to focus more effectively on each task. By setting goals to complete specific tasks within an hour, for example, we learned to focus intensely on our work during a limited time frame and produce results in a shorter period of time.

My approach to thinking about work-life balance is the same as my approach to tidying. Start by visualizing your ideal, identify and cherish those things that spark joy, and let go with gratitude those that don't. If you sense that something's not quite right with your current work-life balance, try asking yourself what would be the perfect balance for you and reexamine the way you want to use your time, referring to the three steps for tidying up work as a couple, introduced on pages 204–206.

Joy at Work Sparks Joy in Life

"My job doesn't give me any kind of social influence. I'm just working to make a living. To talk about work sparking joy is way out of my league."

That's what one of my clients said to me. Some of you who are reading this book may agree with her. But I firmly believe that anyone can make their work spark joy.

When I was five years old, I remember asking my mother, a stay-at-home mom, "Why do you always look so happy when you're doing housework?"

With a smile, she said, "Homemaking is a really important job. Because I cook the meals and keep the house in order, your father can work hard and you can go to school and stay healthy. That's a pretty valuable contribution to society, don't you think? That's why I love my job!" What she said taught me how wonderful the work of a homemaker is. I also learned that people contribute to society in many different ways.

Tidying can make us aware of the vital role that each thing plays in our daily life. We need not just a screwdriver but also screws, no matter how small. Everything, regardless of how insignificant it might seem, has a job to do and works in concert with other things to create and support the home.

Our work is the same. Every job is essential. It doesn't have to be big. Take a good look at your own. How does it contribute to the company as a whole? And how does it contribute to society? Finding meaning in our daily tasks makes our job worth doing, and this leads to joy. In fact, the attitude with which we approach our work is far more important than what kind of job we have. When we're happy and emanating good vibes while we work, as opposed to being stressed and irritable, we have a positive influence on those around us. The greater the number of people like this, the more such positive energy will spread, changing the world. If you radiate joyful energy in the work you do, that in itself is contributing to society.

So tell me, are you enjoying your work?

What kind of working life do you really want?

I'm convinced that tidying is the first and most effective step toward realizing your vision of a joyful career. We hope that you will try the suggestions we offer here for tidying up everything from physical clutter to time, networks, and decision-making. Finish tidying up your workspace, then devote yourself to what you love. Joy at work sparks joy in life.

Marie's Acknowledgments

During interviews, reporters often say, "I'm sure everything in your life must spark joy for you." For years, I couldn't tell them the truth that in my work, this isn't always the case.

The Life-Changing Magic of Tidying Up was first published in Japan in 2010. I was still in my twenties, and somewhere deep inside, I believed that because my message was all about sparking joy through tidying, I had to be Happy Marie, always full of joy. My image of the ideal work life was to relinquish any tedious jobs that didn't spark joy and choose only those that I loved and that connected straight to joy. I thought that every moment at work should be fun.

When I was writing and promoting my book, I really did enjoy my work. Responding to interviews for magazines and television and speaking to large crowds were all new and interesting, and it was thrilling to see book sales rising day by day.

But this lasted only until it was no longer possible to forge ahead by my own efforts alone.

Book sales continued to rise, topping one million copies and then ten million. The KonMari Method spread to other parts of the world. I was named one of *Time* magazine's 100 Most Influential People, moved to the States, started up our company, hosted a Netflix series shown in 190 countries, and even got to walk the red carpet at both the Academy Awards and the Emmy Awards. But as my connections with other people multiplied and the work I was given began to surpass both my volition and my capacity, the pressure and stress sometimes reached a point where my work life didn't always spark joy.

Gradually, I learned how to manage this situation, and I now feel much more comfortable being in the public eye. But to reach this place, I had to overcome plenty of challenges along the way, including in my relations with others and in bridging the gap between reality and my ideal. Writing this book has given me a chance to reflect on the road I have traveled, to reexamine the ups and downs and my mistakes, reminding me that work is not only a way to support my family or contribute to society, but also a channel for personal growth and development.

Over the last decade, I have become far more aware of the value of working with others. Before, I thought that success was something I achieved on my own. Now, however, I am humbled by and grateful for our many amazing collaborators, including our employees in Japan and America, our business partners who work with us on different projects, the KonMari consultants who are active worldwide, and the many fans of the KonMari Method who have embraced our philosophy. Although a little late, I have been learning "on the job" that achievements at work are built upon accumulated effort and in cooperation with others.

Our company vision is to organize the world—to help as many people as we can to finish tidying up and choose what sparks joy for them so that their lives spark joy. We want to spread this vision worldwide. That may sound like an impossible goal, but we're quite serious about achieving it. Just as I spent over two decades developing the KonMari Method to address the difficulties of tidying, we intend to work toward this vision, step by step, for as long as it takes. *Joy at Work* represents a big step toward realizing that dream.

I am profoundly grateful to everyone involved in this project, including my coauthor, Scott, our editor, Tracy, and our agent, Neil, as well as the many clients who shared their tidying stories; my husband, Takumi, whose unstinting professional and personal support is invaluable; and my family. I wish all of you who have chosen to read this book a work life that sparks joy. If what Scott and I have shared here helps you do that, it would make me very happy.

Scott's Acknowledgments

With so much of our time and energy given to work, it can and should be a source of joy. I hope that the research, stories, and guidance we've shared help you realize the career and life changes you deserve. When Marie first reached out to learn about my background, I never would have imagined collaborating to write this book—and with it, having the chance to help so many people gain more happiness, meaning, control, and simply sanity on the job. For someone who has spent almost two decades researching, advising, and teaching people how to make work better, it's a dream come true. I sincerely thank Marie for partnering with me on this journey.

I'm grateful to many people for their help, first and foremost my wife, Randi. Her wisdom and counsel helped make every word I wrote better—and her support and encouragement made finishing the book not just possible but also truly enjoyable. Sharing the experience with her by my side brought us even closer together—and that's a gift that lives beyond these pages.

Two terrific research assistants, Amber Szymczyk and Jessica Yi, arranged the right people to interview, helped locate compelling examples, and conducted test interventions. Additional thanks to Kristen Schwartz for highlighting helpful studies and to Derren Barken for his feedback on digital tidying.

Adam Grant played matchmaker by introducing my work to Marie's team.

Every book needs a champion, and my agent, Richard Pine, skillfully played this role. Beyond his generous comments to push my ideas and edits to make them clearer, the book never would have been finished without his sound judgment and spot-on advice.

My deep appreciation goes to Tracy Behar and the entire Little, Brown Spark team, including Jess Chun, Jules Horbachevsky, Sabrina Callahan, Lauren Hesse, and Ian Straus. Tracy's keen editorial eye and unwavering patience carried the book over—and well past—the finish line.

I'm incredibly lucky to have the support of my colleagues at Rice University. Mikki Hebl and Claudia Kolker provided invaluable comments on the entire manuscript, and Jon Miles offered great insights about teams. I'm also very grateful for the backing from the business school's administration, especially Dean Peter Rodriguez and the entire marketing team, including

Kathleen Clark, Kevin Palmer, and Weezie Mackey. Special thanks to Laurel Smith and Saanya Bhargava for their social media help and to Jeff Falk for assistance with publicity. Nothing sparks more joy for me than having such wonderful colleagues.

Notes

CHAPTER 1: WHY TIDY?

p. 10 **90 percent felt that clutter had a negative impact:** OfficeMax (2011). *2011 Workspace Organization Survey.* http://multivu.prnewswire.com /mnr/officemax/46659/docs/46659-NewsWorthy_Analysis.pdf (accessed 10/11/17).

p. 10 **being surrounded by too many things increases cortisol levels:** Saxbe, D. E., & Repetti, R. (2010). No place like home: Home tours correlate with daily patterns of mood and cortisol. *Personality and Social Psychology Bulletin* 36(1), 71–81.

pp. 10–11 **messy environment taxes the brain:** Kastner, S., & Ungerleider, L. G. (2000). Mechanisms of visual attention in the human cortex. *Annual Review of Neuroscience* 23, 315–41.

p. 11 **half of office workers report mislaying:** Brother International (2010). White paper: *The Costs Associated with Disorganization.* http://www .brother-usa.com/ptouch/meansbusiness/ (accessed 10/9/17).

p. 14 **studies on employee evaluations:** Morrow, P. C., & McElroy, J. C. (1981). Interior office design and visitor response: A constructive replication, *Journal of Applied Psychology* 66(5), 646–50; Campbell,

D. E. (1979). Interior office design and visitor response. *Journal of Applied Psychology* 64(6), 648–53.

p. 16 **messy job setting is more likely to generate creative ideas:** Vohs, K. D., Redden, J. P., & Rahinel, R. (2013). Physical order produces healthy choices, generosity, and conventionality, whereas disorder produces creativity. *Psychological Science* 24(9), 1860–67.

p. 18 **The more stuff...the more overloaded the brain:** Kastner, S., & Ungerleider, L. G. (2000). Mechanisms of visual attention in the human cortex. *Annual Review of Neuroscience* 23, 315–41.

p. 18 **inundated...we lose our sense of control:** Belk, R., Yong Seo, J., & Li, E. (2007). Dirty little secret: Home chaos and professional organizers. *Consumption Markets & Culture* 10, 133–40.

p. 18 **when people feel they are no longer in control, they begin to accumulate:** Raines, A. M., Oglesby, M. E., Unruh, A. S., Capron, D. W., & Schmidt, N. B. (2014). Perceived control: A general psychological vulnerability factor for hoarding. *Personality and Individual Differences* 56, 175–79.

p. 19 **averages 199 unopened emails:** Workfront (2017–2018). *The State of Enterprise Work Report: U.S. Edition.* https://resources.workfront.com /ebooks-whitepapers/2017-2018-state-of-enterprise-work-report -u-s-edition (accessed 10/11/17).

p. 19 **wasting time dealing with unnecessary emails:** Deal, J. J. (2015). White paper: *Always On, Never Done? Don't Blame the Smartphone.* Center for Creative Leadership.

p. 20 **US$420 per employee annually:** https://www.centrify.com/reso urces/5778-centrify-password-survey-summary/ (accessed 05/04/18).

p. 20 **average office worker wastes two hours and thirty-nine minutes:** Erwin, J. (2014, May 29). Email overload is costing you billions— Here's how to crush it. *Forbes.*

p. 20 **dissatisfaction with company meetings:** Perlow, L. A., Hadley, C. N., & Eun, E. (2017, July–Aug). Stop the meeting madness. *Harvard Business Review.* https://hbr.org/2017/07/stop-the-meeting-madness.

p. 20 **more than US$399 billion annually:** https://en.blog.doodle.com/state -of-meeting-2019 (retrieved 12/08/19).

CHAPTER 2: IF YOU KEEP FALLING BACK TO CLUTTER

p. 39 **negative emotions have a more powerful impact:** Averill, J. R. (1980). On the paucity of positive emotions. In Blankstein, K. R., Pliner, P., Polivy, J. (Eds.), *Assessment and Modification of Emotional Behavior. Advances in the Study of Communication and Affect,* vol. 6. Springer, Boston, MA.

CHAPTER 3: TIDYING YOUR WORKSPACE

p. 68 **taking a photo of sentimental items:** Winterich, K. P., Reczek, R. W., & Irwin, Julie R. (2017). Keeping the memory but not the possession: Memory preservation mitigates identity loss from product disposition. *Journal of Marketing* 81(5), 104–20.

CHAPTER 4: TIDYING DIGITAL WORK

p. 83 **prefer to find their files by navigating:** Bergman, O., Whittaker, S., Sanderson, M., Nachmias, R., & Ramamoorthy, A. (2010). The effect of folder structure on personal file navigation. *Journal of the American Society for Information Science and Technology* 61(12), 2426–41.

p. 87 **half his or her day working through emails:** Dewey, C. (2016, October 3). How many hours of your life have you wasted on work email? Try our depressing calculator. *Washington Post.*

p. 87 **email interferes with getting work done:** Workfront (2017–2018). *The State of Enterprise Work Report: U.S. Edition.* https://resources .workfront.com/ebooks-whitepapers/2017-2018-state-of-enterprise -work-report-u-s-edition (accessed 10/11/17).

p. 87 **more time you spend on email, the lower your productivity:** Mark, G., Iqbal, S. T., Czerwinski, M., Johns, P., Sano, A., & Lutchyn, Y. (2016, May). Email duration, batching and self-interruption: Patterns of email use on productivity and stress. In *Proceedings of the 2016 CHI Conference on Human Factors in Computing Systems* (1717–28). New York: ACM Press.

p. 88 **three main ways people tend to approach email:** Whittaker, S., and Sidner, C. (1996). Email overload: Exploring personal information management of email. *Proceedings of CHI '96,* ACM Press, 276–83.

p. 88 **email interruption can require twenty-six minutes:** Iqbal, S. T. and Horvitz, E. (2007). Disruption and recovery of computing tasks: Field study, analysis, and directions. In *Proceedings of the SIGCHI Conference on Human Factors in Computing Systems.* New York: Association for Computing Machinery.

p. 89 **hard to find anything and burdensome to file emails:** Bälter, O. (2000). Keystroke level analysis of email message organization. In *Proceedings of the CHI 2000 Conference on Human Factors in Computing Systems.* New York: ACM Press.

p. 89 **more than twenty folders:** Ibid., 105–12.

p. 94 **average person uses a smartphone eighty-five times a day:** Andrews, S., Ellis, D. A., Shaw, H., & Piwek, L. (2015). Beyond self-report: Tools to compare estimated and real-world smartphone use. *PloS One* 10(10), e0139004.

p. 95 **presence of a smartphone can make you perform poorly:** Ward, A. F., Duke, K., Gneezy, A., & Bos, M. W. (2017). Brain drain: The mere presence of one's own smartphone reduces available cognitive capacity. *Journal of the Association for Consumer Research* 2(2), 140–54.

p. 95 **smartphone during an exam lowered students' grades:** Glass, A. L. & Kang, M. (2018). Dividing attention in the classroom reduces exam performance. *Educational Psychology, 39*(3): 395–408.

p. 96 **phones with them into the bathroom:** https://www.bankmycell.com /blog/cell-phone-usage-in-toilet-survey#jump1 (accessed 6/11/2019).

CHAPTER 5: TIDYING TIME

p. 103 **less than half our workday on our main job responsibilities:** Workfront (2017–2018). *The State of Enterprise Work Report: U.S. Edition.* https://resources.workfront.com/ebooks-whitepapers/2017-2018 -state-of-enterprise-work-report-u-s-edition (accessed 10/11/17).

p. 103 **Overearning:** Hsee, C. K., Zhang, J., Cai, C. F., & Zhang, S. (2013). Overearning. *Psychological Science* 24(6), 852–59.

p. 105 **half of an executive's activities last less than nine minutes:** Mintzberg, H. (1973). *The Nature of Managerial Work.* New York: Harper and Row.

p. 105 **Factory foremen average 583 discrete activities:** Guest, R. H. (1956). Of time and the foreman. *Personnel* 32, 478–86.

p. 105 **one thirty-minute or greater uninterrupted time block:** Stewart, R. (1967). *Managers and Their Jobs.* London: Macmillan.

p. 105 **more than 50 percent of people feel overwhelmed:** ABC News. *Study: U.S. Workers Burned Out.* http://abcnews.go.com/US/story?id =93295&page=1 (accessed 10/11/2017).

p. 107 **pushed around by fake urgency:** Zhu, M., Yang, Y., & Hsee, C. K. (2018, October). The mere urgency effect. *Journal of Consumer Research* 45(3), 673–90.

p. 107 **decreases productivity by as much as 40 percent:** http://www.apa .org/research/action/multitask.aspx (accessed 8/8/18).

p. 108 **rapidly switching from one task to another:** Mark, G., Iqbal, S. T., Czerwinski, M., Johns, P., & Sano, A. (2016, May). Neurotics can't focus: An in situ study of online multitasking in the workplace. In *Proceedings of the 2016 CHI Conference on Human Factors in Computing Systems* (1739–44). New York: ACM Press.

p. 108 **multitaskers don't pay attention:** Ophir, E., Nass, C., & Wagner, A. D. (2009). Cognitive control in media multitaskers. *Proceedings of the National Academy of Sciences of the United States of America* 106(37), 15583–87.

p. 108 **difficulty of the work increases, the downsides of multitasking increase:** Rubinstein, J. S., Meyer, D. E., & Evans, J. E. (2001). Executive control of cognitive processes in task switching. *Journal of Experimental Psychology: Human Perception and Performance* 27(4), 763.

p. 108 **struggle to block out distractions:** Sanbonmatsu, D. M., Strayer, D. L., Medeiros-Ward, N., & Watson, J. M. (2013). Who multi-tasks and why? Multi-tasking ability, perceived multi-tasking ability, impulsivity, and sensation seeking. *PloS One* 8(1), e54402.

p. 109 **reading on paper makes us more carefully evaluate:** Mangen, A. (2017). Textual reading on paper and screens. In A. Black, P. Luna, O. Lund, & S. Walker (Eds.), *Information Design: Research and Practice* (275–89). New York: Routledge.

p. 116 **feel more empowered to say no:** O'Brien, Katharine Ridgway. "Just Saying 'No': An Examination of Gender Differences in the Ability to Decline Requests in the Workplace." PhD diss., Rice University, 2014. https://hdl.handle.net/1911/77421 (accessed 12/11/19).

p. 117 **people make their jobs more satisfying:** Wrzesniewski, A., & Dutton, J. E. (2001). Crafting a job: Revisioning employees as active crafters of their work. *Academy of Management Review* 26(2), 179–201.

p. 117 **to get more done, you sometimes need to work less:** Jett, Q. R., & George, J. M. (2003). Work interrupted: A closer look at the role of interruptions in organizational life. *Academy of Management Review* 28(3), 494–507.

p. 117 **downtime helps you become more creative:** Csikszentmihalyi, M., & Sawyer, K. (1995). Creative insight: The social dimension of a solitary moment. In R. J. Sternberg & J. E. Davidson (Eds.), *The Nature of Insight* (pp. 329–63). Cambridge, MA: MIT Press.

p. 118 **new ways of solving problems:** Elsbach, K. D., & Hargadon, A. B. (2006). Enhancing creativity through "mindless" work: A framework of workday design. *Organization Science* 17(4), 470–83.

CHAPTER 6: TIDYING DECISIONS

p. 120 **thousands of decisions each day:** https://go.roberts.edu/leadingedge/the-great-choices-of-strategic-leaders (accessed 8/22/18).

p. 121 **recall making only about seventy of them:** https://www.ted.com/talks/sheena_iyengar_choosing_what_to_choose/transcript (retrieved 8/22/18).

p. 124 **eats the same breakfast every morning:** https://www.entrepreneur.com/article/244395 (accessed 9/7/18).

p. 129 **For some decisions, people can become overloaded:** Iyengar, S. S., & Lepper, M. R. (2000). When choice is demotivating: Can one desire too much of a good thing? *Journal of Personality and Social Psychology* 79(6), 995–1006.

p. 129 **simple ways to tidy choices:** Scheibehenne, B., Greifeneder, R., & Todd, P. M. (2010). Can there ever be too many options? A meta-analytic review of choice overload. *Journal of Consumer Research* 37(3), 409–25.

p. 130 **if you're unsure of your preferences, more choices can be overwhelming:** Chernev, A. (2003). Product assortment and individual decision processes. *Journal of Personality and Social Psychology* 85(1), 151–62.

p. 131 **overly committed to that solution:** Staw, B. M. (1981). The escalation of commitment to a course of action. *Academy of Management Review* 6(4), 577–87.

CHAPTER 7: TIDYING YOUR NETWORK

p. 136 **make it difficult to form meaningful connections:** Roberts, G. B., Dunbar, R. M., Pollet, T. V., & Kuppens, T. (2009). Exploring variation in active network size: Constraints and ego characteristics, *Social Networks* 31(2),138–46.

p. 136 **150 meaningful connections:** Hill, R. A. & Dunbar, R. I. (2003). Social network size in humans. *Human Nature* 14, 53–72.

p. 136 **interactions come from a small subset of their networks:** https://arxiv.org/abs/0812.1045 (accessed 8/28/18).

p. 137 **more time we spend on social media, the less happy we are:** Kross, E., Verduyn, P., Demiralp, E., et al. (2013, August 14). Facebook use predicts declines in subjective well-being in young adults. *PLoS One, 8*(8): e69841; Lee, S. Y. (2014, March). How do people compare themselves with others on social network sites?: The case of Facebook. *Computers in Human Behavior* 32, 253–60.

p. 142 **two people who genuinely care for each other:** Stephens, J. P., Heaphy, E., & Dutton, J. E. (2011). High-quality connections. In *The Oxford Handbook of Positive Organizational Scholarship* (385–99); Dutton, J. E. (2006). *Energize Your Workplace: How to Create and Sustain High-Quality Connections at Work*. John Wiley & Sons.

pp. 142–143 **quality connections...can contribute to lots of positive out-comes:** Dutton, J. E. (2014). Build high-quality connections. In Dutton, J. E., & Spreitzer, G. M. (Eds.), *How to Be a Positive Leader: Small Actions, Big Impact* (pp. 11–21). San Francisco: Berrett-Koehler Publishers.

p. 145 **deepens our thinking and ignites our creativity:** Mainemelis, C., & Ronson, S. (2006). Ideas are born in fields of play: Towards a theory of play and creativity in organizational settings. *Research in Organizational Behavior* 27, 81–131.

CHAPTER 8: TIDYING MEETINGS

p. 149 **satisfaction with their job is based on satisfaction with the meetings:** Rogelberg, S. G., Allen, J. A., Shanock, L., Scott, C. & Shuffler, M. (2010). Employee satisfaction with meetings: A contemporary facet of job satisfaction. *Human Resource Management* 49(2), 149–72.

p. 149 **greatest obstacles to our productivity:** Workfront (2017–2018). *The State of Enterprise Work Report: U.S. Edition.* https://resources.workfront.com/ebooks-whitepapers/2017-2018-state-of-enterprise-work-report-u-s-edition (accessed 10/11/17)

p. 149 **emotionally exhaust us:** Lehmann-Willenbrock, N., Allen, J. A., & Belyeu, D. (2016). Our love/hate relationship with meetings: Relating good and bad meeting behaviors to meeting outcomes, engagement, and exhaustion. *Management Research Review* 39(10), 1293–1312.

p. 154 **providing an explanation...will boost your chances:** Langer, E. J., Blank, A., & Chanowitz, B. (1978). The mindlessness of ostensibly thoughtful action: The role of "placebic" information in interpersonal interaction. *Journal of Personality and Social Psychology* 36(6), 635–42.

p. 156 **talking provides the same feelings...as eating or having sex:** Tamir, D. I., & Mitchell, J. P. (2012). Disclosing information about the self is intrinsically rewarding. *Proceedings of the National Academy of Sciences* 109(21), 8038–43.

p. 157 **bad meeting behavior did much more harm:** Kauffeld, S., & Lehmann-Willenbrock, N. (2012). Meetings matter: Effects of team meetings on team and organizational success. *Small Group Research* 43(2), 130–58.

p. 159 **slows down decision-making:** Smith, K. G., Smith, K. A., Olian, J. D., Sims Jr, H. P., O'Bannon, D. P., & Scully, J. A. (1994). Top management team demography and process: The role of social integration and communication. *Administrative Science Quarterly* 39(3), 412–38.

p. 159 **lowers productivity:** Karr-Wisniewski, P., & Lu, Y. (2010). When more is too much: Operationalizing technology overload and exploring its impact on knowledge worker productivity. *Computers in Human Behavior* 26, 1061–72.

p. 159 **leads to worse decisions:** Kerr, N. L., & Tindale, R. S. (2004). Group performance and decision making. *Annual Review of Psychology* 55, 623–55.

p. 161 **more meetings didn't increase productivity:** Luong, A., & Rogelberg, S. G. (2005). Meetings and more meetings: The relationship between meeting load and the daily well-being of employees. *Group Dynamics: Theory, Research, and Practice* 9(1), 58–67.

p. 161 **"standing" meetings...lead to more creative ideas and more collaboration:** Knight, A. P., & Baer, M. (2014). Get up, stand up: The effects of a non-sedentary workspace on information elaboration and group performance. *Social Psychological and Personality Science* 5(8), 910–17.

p. 161 **standing meetings tend to be shorter:** Taparia, N. (2014, June 19). Kick the chair: How standing cut our meeting times by 25%. *Forbes.*

CHAPTER 9: TIDYING TEAMS

p. 168 **a team of hospital cleaners:** Wrzesniewski, A., & Dutton, J. E. (2001). Crafting a job: Revisioning employees as active crafters of their work. *Academy of Management Review* 26(2), 179–201.

p. 171 **trusting one another helps people avoid burning out:** Harvey, S., Kelloway, E. K., & Duncan-Leiper, L. (2003). Trust in management as a buffer of the relationships between overload and strain. *Journal of Occupational Health Psychology* 8(4), 306.

p. 172 **efforts go toward individual goals:** Dirks, K. T. (1999). The effects of interpersonal trust on work group performance. *Journal of Applied Psychology* 84(3), 445–55.

p. 173 **everyone knows in common:** Gigone, D., & Hastie, R. (1993). The common knowledge effect: Information sharing and group judgment. *Journal of Personality and Social Psychology* 65(5), 959–74.

p. 173 **small bits of information:** Stasser, G., & Titus, W. (1985). Pooling of unshared information in group decision making: Biased information sampling during discussion. *Journal of Personality and Social Psychology* 48(6), 1467–78.

p. 174 **brainwriting:** VanGundy, A. B. (1984). Brainwriting for new product ideas: An alternative to brainstorming. *Journal of Consumer Marketing* 1(2), 67–74.

p. 175 **Trust turns disagreements over ideas into productive conversations:** Simons, T. L., & Peterson, R. S. (2000). Task conflict and relationship conflict in top management teams: The pivotal role of intragroup trust. *Journal of Applied Psychology* 85(1), 102–11.

p. 175 **egocentric orientation:** Weingart, L. R., Brett, J. M., Olekalns, M., & Smith, P. L. (2007). Conflicting social motives in negotiating groups. *Journal of Personality and Social Psychology* 93(6), 994–1010.

p. 176 **optimal size for most teams:** Hackman, J. R., & Vidmar, N. (1970). Effects of size and task type on group performance and member reactions. *Sociometry, 37*–54; Hackman, J. R. (2002). *Leading Teams: Setting the Stage for Great Performances.* Harvard Business Press.

CHAPTER 10: SHARING THE MAGIC OF TIDYING

p. 182 **the messy one had three times as much additional clutter:** Ramos, J. & Torgler, B. (2012). Are academics messy? Testing the broken windows theory with a field experiment in the work environment. *Review of Law and Economics* 8(3), 563–77.

p. 185 **survey of two thousand Americans:** https://greatergood.berkeley.edu /images/uploads/GratitudeFullResults_FINAL1pdf.pdf (accessed 6/7/19).

p. 185 **receiving gratitude makes employees more engaged:** Fehr, R., Zheng, X., Jiwen Song, L., Guo, Y., & Ni, D. (2019). Thanks for everything: A quasi-experimental field study of expressing and receiving gratitude. Working paper.

CHAPTER 11: HOW TO SPARK EVEN MORE JOY AT WORK

p. 201 **we remember the bad ones:** Baumeister, R. F., Bratslavsky, E., Finkenauer, C., & Vohs, K. D. (2001). Bad is stronger than good. *Review of General Psychology* 5(4), 323–70.

p. 201 **imagined failure puts us on a course to fail:** Stoeber, J., Hutchfield, J., & Wood, K. V. (2007). Perfectionism, self-efficacy, and aspiration level: Differential effects of perfectionistic striving and self-criticism after success and failure. *Personality and Individual Differences* 45(4), 323–27.

Index

About the Authors

Marie Kondo is a tidying expert, best-selling author, Emmy-nominated television star, and founder of KonMari Media, Inc.

Enchanted with organizing since her childhood, Marie began her tidying-consultant business as a nineteen-year-old university student in Tokyo. Today she is a world-renowned tidying expert and pop-culture icon helping people to transform their cluttered homes into spaces of serenity and inspiration.

Marie has been named one of *Time* magazine's 100 Most Influential People, and her work has been featured in thousands of international publications, radio programs, and major television shows.

Scott Sonenshein is the Henry Gardiner Symonds Professor of Management at Rice University. He holds a PhD in organizational behavior from the University of Michigan, an MPhil from the University of Cambridge, and a BA from the University of Virginia. His award-winning research, teaching, and speaking helps people experience greater meaning, satisfaction, and success by unlocking their creativity and resourcefulness. Scott previously worked as a strategy consultant before joining a Silicon Valley startup's marketing group. He has written for the *New York Times, Time* magazine, *Fast Company,* and *Harvard Business Review.*